The Illmatic Investor

From Hip-Hop to High Returns

The Art of Building Wealth through Stocks, Startups, and Strategic Investments Inspired by Nas & His Queensbridge Venture Fund

By Ash Cash

First published in the United States of America.

DISCLAIMER

The advice contained in this material might not be suitable for everyone. The author designed the information to present his opinion about the subject matter. The reader must carefully investigate all aspects of any business decision before committing to him or herself. The author obtained the information contained herein from sources he believes to be reliable and from his own personal experience, but he neither implies nor intends any guarantee of accuracy. The author is not in the business of giving legal, accounting, or any other type of professional advice. Should the reader need such advice, he or she must seek services from a competent professional. The author particularly disclaims any liability, loss, or risk taken by individuals who directly or indirectly act on the information contained herein. The author believes the advice presented here is sound, but readers cannot hold him responsible for either the actions they take, or the risk taken by individuals who directly or indirectly act on the information contained herein.

Published by 1BrickPublishing
Printed in the United States

ISBN 978-1949303568

DEDICATION

This book is dedicated to the dreamers and hustlers who refuse to be defined by their circumstances, who see obstacles as opportunities, and who never stop believing in the power of their own potential. To those who understand that hip-hop is not just a music genre but a powerful teaching tool, and who are ready to use the wisdom and lessons embedded in its lyrics and culture to build a strong financial foundation and unlock their own greatness. May this book serve as a source of inspiration and guidance on your journey towards abundance and prosperity.

DEDICATION REQUEST

Please share this book with anyone who you feel would benefit from its guidance, inspiration, and actionable steps for navigating the world of investing and building long-term wealth. Together, we can spread the message of financial empowerment and help others unlock the abundance that is rightfully theirs.

TABLE OF CONTENTS

INTRODUCTION

THE GENESIS OF ILLMATIC INVESTING

"Street's disciple, my raps are trifle I shoot slugs from my brain just like a rifle."

Picture this: it's 1994 in New York City. The streets are pulsing with a raw, unbridled energy. The city is a melting pot of cultures, a disharmony of sounds and styles. Boom baps echo from street corners as b-boys and b-girls lay down cardboard to break dance. Graffiti artists leave their mark on subway cars and brick walls, while the fashion is a mix of baggy jeans, Timberland boots, and oversized sneakers. The World Trade Center towers stand tall, iconic symbols of the city's resilience and ambition.

But beneath the surface, tensions are simmering. The crack epidemic of the '80s has left deep scars on communities of color, and the Rodney King beating, and subsequent LA riots have shone a harsh light on police brutality and racial injustice. In the midst of this turmoil, a young kid from the Queensbridge Houses is about to drop an album that will change the face of hip-hop forever. Nas' "Illmatic" is a searing, poetic portrait of life in the city's forgotten corners, a testament to the power of art to reflect and transform the world around us. Little does he know that, 30 years later, he'll be at the forefront of another revolution – this time, in the world of tech and venture capital. The stage is set for a story that will transcend time and place, a story of hustle, heart, and the relentless pursuit of a dream.

As a 13-year-old kid from Harlem when Nas' groundbreaking album "Illmatic" dropped on April 19, 1994, I couldn't have imagined the profound impact it would have, not only on hip-hop, but on my own journey as a financial educator. Now, with over two decades of experience under my belt, it's an absolute honor to draw parallels between the world of music and finance through the lens of Nas' remarkable transition from legendary MC to savvy tech investor.

Nas' venture into the world of startups and investing through his Queensbridge Venture Partners fund is a testament to his visionary mindset. Co-founded with Anthony Saleh, Queensbridge Venture Partners (QVP) has consistently demonstrated a keen ability to identify and capitalize on key trends in highly competitive markets. By focusing on co-investment opportunities alongside leading venture capital funds and angel investors in Silicon Valley, Nas and his team have secured access to some of the most promising companies in the tech space.

It's this strategic approach, coupled with Nas' innate hustle and creativity, that has propelled him to astonishing heights in the world of business. From early investments in Dropbox and Lyft to his stakes in Ring and PillPack, which were eventually acquired by Amazon for a combined sum of over $1 billion, Nas has proven time and again that he has an eye for spotting winners.

But it's not just about the money for Nas. Just as his music has always been a reflection of his roots and his community, his investments are driven by a desire to empower and uplift. Through QVP, he's not only creating wealth for himself, but he's opening doors and creating opportunities for others.

As someone who's dedicated my career to helping others navigate the often-intimidating world of finance, I can't help but be inspired by Nas' journey. He's shown us that with hard work, determination, and a willingness to take calculated risks, anyone can achieve financial success - regardless of where they come from.

This book, "The Illmatic Investor," is a celebration of that journey and a guide for those who wish to follow in Nas's footsteps. It's a roadmap for navigating the complex world of investing, drawing parallels between the principles of hip-hop and the strategies needed for financial success.

At its core, hip-hop is about storytelling, about painting a picture with words and beats. It's about taking your lived experiences and translating them into art that resonates with others. Investing, in many ways, follows a similar path. It's about understanding the story behind a company, about seeing the potential in an idea and having the courage to back it.

Nas's approach to investing is deeply rooted in his hip-hop background. He brings the same level of creativity, hustle, and street smarts to the world of finance as he does to his music. He's not afraid to take risks, but he also knows the importance of diversification and strategic planning.

Throughout the book, we won't just draw inspiration from Nas's lyrical genius. I, Ash Cash, known as the Hip-Hop Financial Advisor and one of the world's top financial educators, will be your guide, providing additional insight and perspective. My expertise will enrich our understanding of what it takes to be a successful investor, as I break down complex financial concepts and share practical strategies that have helped countless individuals build wealth. With my unique blend of hip-hop culture and financial acumen, I'll make the journey to financial success both engaging and accessible.

But this isn't just a book about Nas. It's a book about the power of investing to change lives and communities. It's about the potential for hip-hop culture to inform and inspire a new generation of investors. It's about the idea that no matter where you come from, with the right knowledge and mindset, you can achieve financial freedom.

In Part I, "Laying Down the Beats," we dive into the fundamentals of investing. Just as a great hip-hop track needs a solid beat, a successful investment strategy needs a strong foundation. We start with "NY State of Mind," a chapter that breaks down the basics of the stock market, using Nas's lyrics to illustrate key concepts. From there, we move on to "Life's a B**ch," which tackles the crucial topic of risk management and diversification, drawing lessons from Nas's own investment choices. We close out this section with "The World Is Yours," a guide to identifying and seizing investment opportunities.

Part II, "The Startup Symphony," takes us into the exciting and unpredictable world of startup investing. This is where Nas has truly made his mark in recent years, with Queensbridge Venture Partners backing a number of high-profile startups. In "Halftime," we learn how to evaluate startups like a pro, using Nas's own approach as a model. "One Love" explores the importance of building relationships in the startup world, while "It Ain't Hard to Tell" tracks the journey from startup to success, highlighting stories from Nas's own portfolio.

Finally, in Part III, "Strategic Investments," we broaden our horizons, looking at ways to diversify beyond the basics of stocks and startups. "Represent" dives into the world of real estate and alternative investments, using Nas's own diversification strategies as a guide. In "Memory Lane," we take a thoughtful look at the inevitable failures and successes of investing, stressing the importance of resilience in the face of setbacks.

In the Conclusion, "If I Ruled the World," we'll bring all of these threads together, envisioning what your financial future could look like if you apply the lessons of the Illmatic Investor. We'll talk about setting long-term financial goals and staying true to your roots and values even as you navigate the complex world of investing.

Investing, like hip-hop, is not just about individual success. It's about building something larger than yourself. It's about using your resources and your platform to make a difference in your community and in the world.

Nas's journey is proof that these worlds are not as far apart as they seem. With the right mindset, the right strategies, and the right team in your corner, you can achieve the kind of success that once seemed like a distant dream.

So whether you're a hip-hop head looking to make your first investment, or a seasoned investor looking for a fresh perspective, this book is for you. Get ready to lay down some beats, to build your own startup symphony, to make strategic moves that will set you up for long-term success.

Get ready to become an Illmatic Investor.

PART I: LAYING DOWN THE BEATS - FUNDAMENTALS OF INVESTING

CHAPTER 1

NY STATE OF MIND - UNDERSTANDING THE STOCK MARKET

"Be havin' dreams that I'm a gangsta, drinkin' Moëts, holdin' TEC's Makin' sure the cash came correct, then I stepped Investments in stock, sewin' up the blocks to sell rocks."

The streets of New York in the 1990s were a world unto themselves - a gritty, vibrant, and often unforgiving landscape that shaped a generation of artists, hustlers, and visionaries. It was a time when hip-hop was more than just music; it was a way of life, a means of expression, and a ticket out of the struggle. And for a young Nasir Jones, better known to the world as Nas, those streets were both a source of inspiration and a battlefield to be conquered.

To understand Nas, his business moves, and how to become an Illmatic Investor, you first have to understand what it means to have a "NY State of Mind." Having a "NY State of Mind" is a mentality that embodies the grit, hustle, and relentless pursuit of success that is synonymous with the city of New York. It's a mindset that has been forged in the crucible of the city's unforgiving streets, where only the strong survive and the weak are left behind.

To have a "NY State of Mind" is to possess an unshakeable belief in oneself, a willingness to take risks, and a determination to succeed no matter the odds.

In the world of Wall Street, having a "NY State of Mind" is essential for navigating the cutthroat world of finance. The stock market is a high-stakes game where fortunes can be made or lost in the blink of an eye, and only those with the gall and a solid understanding of the game can hope to come out on top. To succeed on Wall Street, one must be able to think quickly, adapt to changing market conditions, and make bold moves when the time is right. It requires a level of mental toughness and emotional resilience that can only be forged through years of experience and hard-won lessons.

Similarly, in the street life, having a "NY State of Mind" is a matter of survival. The streets of New York can be a harsh and unforgiving place, where danger lurks around every corner and trust is a rare commodity. To navigate this world successfully, one must be street-smart, quick-witted, and always on the lookout for opportunities to get ahead. It requires a level of situational awareness and adaptability that can only be honed through years of living on the edge.

In the music industry, having a "NY State of Mind" is what separates the legends from the one-hit wonders. The music business is a notoriously fickle and competitive world, where success is often fleeting and the pressure to stay relevant is constant. To make it in this industry, one must have an unshakeable belief in their own talent, a willingness to put in the hard work and long hours, and a determination to keep pushing forward no matter the obstacles. It requires a level of creativity, hustle, and business savvy that can only be honed through years of grinding and perfecting one's craft.

What ties all of these worlds together is the common thread of the "NY State of Mind" - the unshakeable belief in oneself, the willingness to take risks, and the determination to succeed no matter the odds. Whether you're a trader on Wall Street, a hustler on the streets, or an artist in the studio, having a "NY State of Mind" is what sets you apart from the rest. It's the secret sauce that fuels the engine of success in the city that never sleeps, and it's what has made New York the center of the universe for generations of dreamers and doers alike.

Nas embodies this "NY State of Mind" in all aspects of his life and career. From his early days hustling on the streets of Queensbridge to his rise to the top of the rap game, Nas has always approached life with a level of intensity and determination that is quintessentially New York, so in other words "Nas stays on his NY ish" (Swizz Beatz voice). He has navigated the cutthroat world of the music industry with the same street-smart savvy and adaptability that he honed on the streets, and has emerged as one of the most respected and influential rappers of his generation or dare I say of ALL times.

In his later years, Nas has brought that same "NY State of Mind" to the world of business and investing, using his keen eye for opportunity and his relentless drive to succeed to build a portfolio of successful ventures and investments.

At the end of the day, having a "NY State of Mind" is about more than just being from New York - it's about embodying the spirit of the city in all that you do. It's about having the courage to take risks, the resilience to bounce back from setbacks, and the determination to keep pushing forward no matter the odds. Whether you're a rapper, a trader, or a hustler on the streets, having a "NY State of Mind" is what sets you apart from the rest - and it's what has made Nas one of the most enduring and influential figures in hip-hop history.

Born in 1973 in Brooklyn and raised in the Queensbridge housing projects in Long Island City, Queens, Nas grew up in the heart of the city's burgeoning hip-hop scene. He witnessed firsthand the raw energy and entrepreneurial spirit that drove the culture forward, from the DJ battles and graffiti-covered subway cars to the makeshift recording studios and hustlers on the corner. It was a world where creativity, grit, and a keen understanding of the game could take you from the bottom to the top - a concept that would later translate seamlessly into Nas' approach to the stock market.

Nas's journey from the streets of Queensbridge to the pinnacle of hip-hop success is a testament to his unwavering dedication, lyrical prowess, and ability to adapt to the ever-changing landscape of the music industry. His debut album, Illmatic (1994), is widely regarded as one of the greatest hip-hop albums of all time, showcasing his exceptional storytelling skills and poetic flow. The album's raw, gritty depiction of life in the projects resonated with listeners and established Nas as a force to be reckoned with in the rap game.

Throughout his career, Nas has consistently pushed the boundaries of the genre, exploring a wide range of themes and styles in his music. From the introspective and socially conscious tracks on It Was Written (1996) and I Am... (1999) to the politically charged and controversial untitled album (2008), Nas has never shied away from tackling complex issues and challenging societal norms.

Beyond his music career, Nas has also made a name for himself as a savvy businessman and investor. In 2013, he founded QueensBridge Venture Partners, a venture capital firm that has made successful investments in a wide range of startups, including Coinbase, Lyft, and Dropbox. Nas's keen eye for emerging trends and his ability to identify promising investment opportunities have helped establish him as a respected figure in the tech industry.

In his personal life, Nas has faced his share of challenges and triumphs. He married singer Kelis in 2005, but the couple divorced in 2010. Nas is the father of two children, a daughter named Destiny and a son named Knight. Despite the ups and downs of his personal relationships, Nas has remained committed to his family and has often spoken about the importance of being a present and supportive father.

Throughout his decades-long career, Nas has remained a vital and influential presence in the hip-hop world. His later albums, such as Life Is Good (2012) the King's Disease series (2020-2022), The Magic Series (2021-2023), as well as a collaboration album with DJ Premier (2024) have showcased his ability to evolve and adapt his sound while still maintaining the lyrical depth and storytelling prowess that have defined his career. With a legacy that spans over three decades, Nas continues to inspire and influence new generations of rappers and fans alike, cementing his status as a true icon of hip-hop culture.

To make it this far, Nas had to navigate the complex web of relationships, rivalries, and power dynamics that defined the street life and his music career, and in similar fashion a trader must navigate the intricate landscape of the stock market. In all three worlds, knowledge is power, and the ability to read people, anticipate moves, and adapt to changing circumstances can mean the difference between success and failure.

The stock market, like the hip-hop industry, is a game of hustle and flow. It's about identifying opportunities, taking calculated risks, and making strategic moves to come out on top. Just as Nas had to learn the rules of the street to survive and thrive, a trader must learn the fundamentals of the market - the players, the terminology, the patterns, and the pitfalls.

At its core, the stock market is a platform where shares of publicly traded companies are bought and sold. When Nas was coming up in the '90s, the hip-hop business was still in its infancy, with artists and labels figuring out how to monetize the culture and build sustainable brands. Similarly, for a new trader, the stock market can seem like a daunting and complex beast, full of unfamiliar terms and concepts.

But just as Nas studied the greats who came before him - the likes of Rakim, Kool G Rap, and Big Daddy Kane - to hone his craft, a trader must study the market, learning from the successes and failures of those who came before. And just as Nas had to find his own voice and style to stand out in a crowded field, a trader must develop their own strategy and approach, based on their unique goals, risk tolerance, and market outlook.

One of the key concepts in trading is the idea of buying low and selling high - essentially, identifying undervalued assets, investing in them, and then selling them off at a profit when their value rises. This concept is not unlike the street hustle of flipping products - buying low, adding value, and selling high. It's about having a keen eye for opportunity and the patience and discipline to see it through.

In the stock market, as in the hip-hop game, timing is everything. Nas didn't become a legend overnight; he put in the work, paid his dues, and waited for his moment to shine. Similarly, a trader must be patient, watching the market closely for the right entry and exit points, and not letting emotions like fear or greed cloud their judgment.

Another key parallel between the street life and the stock market is the importance of diversification. In the '90s, the most successful hip-hop moguls were those who expanded beyond just the music, branching out into fashion, film, and other ventures. They understood that relying on a single revenue stream was risky, and that by diversifying their portfolio, they could weather the ups and downs of the industry.

The same principle applies in trading. By spreading your investments across a variety of asset classes, sectors, and individual securities, you can mitigate risk and maximize your chances of success. Just as Nas couldn't put all his eggs in one basket, relying solely on his music career, a trader shouldn't put all their capital into a single stock or sector.

Of course, no discussion of the stock market would be complete without addressing the element of risk. The streets of '90s New York were a high-stakes environment, where one false move could have serious consequences. The same is true of the stock market - every trade carries with it the potential for loss, and it's up to the individual trader to manage that risk through careful research, strategic planning, and disciplined execution.

For Nas, risk management meant staying alert, trusting his instincts, and always having a backup plan. He knew that the game could change at any moment, and that the key to survival was adaptability. In the stock market, risk management involves setting clear stop-loss orders, diversifying your portfolio, and staying disciplined in your approach, even in the face of market volatility or emotional temptation.

This is why having a "NY State of Mind" is so important. Nas didn't let the obstacles in his path define him; he used them as fuel for his ambition, crafting vivid narratives of struggle and triumph that resonated with millions.

Similarly, a successful trader must approach the market with mental toughness, seeing challenges as opportunities and never losing sight of the bigger picture. They must be willing to think outside the box, to take calculated risks, and to bounce back from inevitable setbacks. They must be students of the game, constantly learning, adapting, and evolving their approach.

In the end, the journey from the streets of Queensbridge to the top of the stock market is not for the faint of heart. It requires hustle, intelligence, and a certain fearlessness in the face of uncertainty. But for those who embrace the grind, who approach the market with the same hunger and determination that drove Nas to become one of the greatest rappers of all time, the rewards can be life-changing.

So as you dive into the world of stock trading, take a page from Nas' playbook. Study the greats, find your own voice, and never stop hustling. The market, like the streets, is always watching, always testing, always separating the contenders from the pretenders. But with the right mindset, the right strategy, and the right team in your corner, there's no limit to how far you can go.

What is the Stock Market?

At its core, the stock market is a platform where shares of publicly traded companies are bought and sold. When a company decides to go public, it offers a portion of its ownership in the form of stocks. These stocks are then traded on exchanges, such as the New York Stock Exchange (NYSE) or the NASDAQ.

By buying a stock, you're essentially purchasing a small piece of the company, becoming a shareholder. As a shareholder, you have the potential to profit in two ways: through dividends (a portion of the company's earnings distributed to shareholders) and through capital appreciation (an increase in the stock's price).

The stock market serves as a vital component of the global economy, allowing companies to raise capital for growth and expansion while providing investors with opportunities to grow their wealth.

Market Participants

The stock market is a complex ecosystem with a variety of participants, each with their own goals, strategies, and levels of expertise. Some of the key players include:

1. Individual Investors: Also known as retail investors, these are everyday people who buy and sell stocks for their personal portfolios. They may be long-term investors saving for retirement or short-term traders looking to capitalize on market movements.

2. Institutional Investors: These are large organizations such as mutual funds, pension funds, hedge funds, and insurance companies that pool

together money from multiple investors to make significant investments in the stock market.

3. Market Makers: These are firms that facilitate trading by always being ready to buy or sell a particular stock at the quoted bid and ask prices. They help ensure liquidity in the market.

4. Brokers: These are licensed professionals or firms that act as intermediaries between buyers and sellers, executing trades on behalf of their clients.

Understanding Stock Prices

One of the most important concepts to grasp in stock trading is how stock prices are determined. At the most basic level, stock prices are driven by supply and demand. When more people want to buy a stock (high demand), the price goes up. Conversely, when more people want to sell a stock (high supply), the price goes down.

However, numerous factors can influence supply and demand, and consequently, stock prices. Some of these factors include:

1. Company Performance: A company's financial health, growth prospects, and overall management can significantly impact its stock price. Strong earnings reports, innovative products, and positive news can drive stock prices up, while missed earnings targets, scandals, or poor management can send prices tumbling.

2. Economic Conditions: The overall state of the economy, including factors such as GDP growth, inflation, interest rates, and unemployment, can affect stock prices. Generally, a strong economy with low unemployment and steady growth is good for the stock market, while economic downturns and recessions can lead to market declines.

3. Market Sentiment: The overall mood and confidence of investors can have a significant impact on stock prices. When investors are optimistic and bullish, they're more likely to buy stocks, driving prices up. When they're pessimistic and bearish, they may sell off stocks, leading to price drops.

4. Global Events: Political upheavals, natural disasters, pandemics, and other global events can all have ripple effects on the stock market. For example, a major geopolitical conflict could disrupt global trade and lead to market volatility.

Types of Stock Trading

There are several approaches to stock trading, each with its own strategies, time horizons, and risk profiles. Some common types include:

1. Day Trading: This involves buying and selling stocks within the same trading day, with the goal of profiting from short-term price movements. Day traders often make multiple trades in a single day and aim to end the day with no open positions.

2. Swing Trading: Swing traders hold stocks for a few days to a few weeks, attempting to profit from short-term to medium-term price swings. They often use technical analysis to identify trading opportunities.

3. Position Trading: Position traders take a longer-term approach, holding stocks for months or even years. They often base their decisions on a company's fundamental strength and growth prospects, aiming to profit from long-term appreciation.

4. Momentum Trading: Momentum traders look to capitalize on stocks or markets showing strong directional momentum. They attempt to buy high and sell even higher (or short sell low and buy back even lower).

5. Value Investing: Value investors seek out stocks that appear undervalued by the market, with the expectation that the stock price will eventually rise to reflect the company's true worth. This approach often involves in-depth fundamental analysis.

Market Orders vs Limit Orders

When it comes to executing trades, there are two main types of orders: market orders and limit orders.

A market order is an order to buy or sell a stock at the best available current market price. When you place a market order, you're essentially saying, "I want to buy/sell this stock right now, at whatever the current price is." Market orders are typically executed immediately (assuming there are willing buyers or sellers), but the price you get may differ from the last-traded price, especially in fast-moving markets.

On the other hand, a limit order is an order to buy or sell a stock at a specific price or better. When you place a buy limit order, you're saying, "I want to buy this stock, but only at this price or lower." When you place a sell limit order, you're saying, "I want to sell this stock, but only at this price or higher." Limit orders give you more control over the price at which your trade is executed, but there's no guarantee that your order will be filled, especially if the stock doesn't reach the specified price.

Bull Markets vs Bear Markets

The stock market goes through cycles of ups and downs, referred to as bull markets and bear markets.

A bull market is characterized by a sustained period of rising stock prices, typically by 20% or more from recent lows. Bull markets are often driven by strong economic growth, high investor confidence, and positive market sentiment. During bull markets, investors tend to be more optimistic and willing to take on more risk.

Conversely, a bear market is defined as a prolonged period of declining stock prices, typically by 20% or more from recent highs. Bear markets are often associated with economic downturns, recessions, high unemployment, and negative market sentiment. During bear markets, investors tend to be more pessimistic and risk-averse.

It's important to note that even within bull and bear markets, there can be short-term pullbacks (in a bull market) or rallies (in a bear market). These are often referred to as market corrections.

Diversification

One of the key principles of successful investing is diversification – spreading your investments across a variety of asset classes, sectors, and individual securities. The goal of diversification is to minimize risk and volatility in your portfolio.

Think of it this way: if you put all your money into a single stock, and that stock performs poorly, your entire investment is at risk. But if you spread your money across many different stocks, bonds, and other assets, the impact of any single investment's poor performance is lessened.

Some common ways to diversify your portfolio include:

1. Investing across different asset classes: This means holding a mix of stocks, bonds, cash, and possibly alternative investments like real estate or commodities.

2. Investing across different sectors: Rather than concentrating your investments in a single industry, you might hold stocks from the technology sector, healthcare sector, financial sector, and so on.

3. Investing across different geographies: You might hold domestic stocks as well as international stocks to gain exposure to different economies and markets.

4. Investing in different company sizes: You might hold a mix of large-cap, mid-cap, and small-cap stocks.

The key is to find a balance that aligns with your investment goals, risk tolerance, and time horizon.

Fundamental Analysis

Fundamental analysis is the process of evaluating a company's financial health and growth prospects to determine its intrinsic value. The goal is to identify stocks that are undervalued by the market and have the potential for long-term growth.

Some of the key factors considered in fundamental analysis include:

1. Revenue and Earnings: Analysts look at a company's revenue (total sales) and earnings (profits) over time. Consistent growth in these metrics is generally a positive sign.

2. Profit Margins: This is the amount of profit a company generates per dollar of sales. Higher profit margins can indicate a competitive advantage or efficient operations.

3. Debt Levels: Too much debt can be a red flag, as it can limit a company's flexibility and increase its risk of financial distress.

4. Competitive Advantage: Analysts look for companies with a unique selling proposition or competitive moat that can help them maintain market share and profitability.

5. Management Quality: The expertise, vision, and integrity of a company's management team can greatly impact its long-term success.

6. Industry Trends: Understanding the broader trends and growth prospects of the industry a company operates in is crucial to evaluating its potential.

Fundamental analysis often involves diving into a company's financial statements, including the income statement, balance sheet, and cash flow statement. It also involves keeping up with company news, industry developments, and economic trends.

Technical Analysis

While fundamental analysis focuses on a company's underlying business, technical analysis takes a different approach. Technical analysts study historical price and volume data to identify patterns and trends that can suggest future price movements.

Some common tools and concepts in technical analysis include:

1. Price Charts: Technical analysts use various types of charts (such as line charts, bar charts, and candlestick charts) to visualize price movements over time.

2. Trend Lines: By connecting a series of price highs or lows, analysts can identify uptrends (higher highs and higher lows) or downtrends (lower highs and lower lows).

3. Support and Resistance Levels: These are price levels where the stock has had difficulty moving beyond in the past. A support level is a price level where the stock has tended to stop falling and bounce back up. A resistance level is a price level where the stock has tended to stop rising and pull back down.

4. Moving Averages: These are trend-following indicators that smooth out price data by creating a constantly updated average price. Common moving averages include the 50-day and 200-day moving averages.

5. Oscillators: These are momentum indicators that help identify overbought or oversold conditions in a stock. Examples include the Relative Strength Index (RSI) and the Stochastic Oscillator.

Technical analysts believe that price movements often follow patterns and that by studying past price behavior, it's possible to predict future price behavior. However, it's important to note that technical analysis is not an exact science and should be used in conjunction with other forms of analysis and risk management strategies.

Risk Management

No discussion of stock trading would be complete without addressing risk management. The stock market can be volatile and unpredictable, and even the most promising investments can turn sour. That's why it's crucial to have a solid risk management plan in place.

Some key components of a risk management strategy include:

1. Setting Stop-Losses: A stop-loss is a predetermined price level at which you'll sell a stock to limit your losses if the price drops. This can help prevent small losses from turning into big ones.

2. Position Sizing: This involves determining how much of your capital to allocate to each trade based on your risk tolerance and the trade's potential reward. A common rule of thumb is to risk no more than 1-2% of your capital on any single trade.

3. Diversification: As mentioned earlier, diversifying your portfolio across different assets, sectors, and geographies can help mitigate risk.

4. Hedging: This involves using financial instruments (such as options or futures contracts) to reduce the risk of adverse price movements in your holdings.

5. Staying Disciplined: Having a trading plan and sticking to it, even in the face of market volatility or emotional temptation, is key to managing risk. This includes setting clear entry and exit points for your trades and avoiding impulsive decisions based on fear or greed.

Remember, the goal of risk management is not to eliminate risk entirely (which is impossible), but to manage it in a way that allows you to stay in the game for the long run.

The Psychology of Trading

Beyond the technical aspects of stock trading, there's another crucial factor to consider: your own psychology. The markets are driven by the collective decisions of millions of participants, each with their own emotions, biases, and risk tolerances.

Some common psychological pitfalls that traders face include:

1. Fear and Greed: The fear of missing out (FOMO) can lead traders to chase after hot stocks or trends, while the fear of losing money can cause them to sell prematurely. On the flip side, greed can lead to excessive risk-taking or holding onto losing positions too long.

2. Confirmation Bias: This is the tendency to seek out information that confirms our existing beliefs and ignore information that contradicts it. In trading, this can lead to holding onto losing positions or doubling down on bad decisions.

3. Overconfidence: Successful trades can lead to a false sense of invincibility, causing traders to take on too much risk or neglect proper due diligence.

4. Herd Mentality: The temptation to follow the crowd can be strong, especially in bull markets or during periods of market hype. But just because everyone else is buying (or selling) doesn't mean it's the right decision for you.

To be a successful trader, it's important to be aware of these psychological traps and develop strategies to mitigate them. This might include:

- Setting clear, objective rules for your trades and sticking to them.

- Keeping a trading journal to track your decisions and learn from your mistakes.

- Taking breaks and stepping away from the markets when emotions are running high.

- Continuously educating yourself and staying humble.

Remember, trading is as much a mental game as it is a financial one.

Continuous Learning

The world of stock trading is vast and ever-changing. New companies emerge, industries evolve, and market dynamics shift. To stay ahead of the curve, it's crucial to adopt a mindset of continuous learning.

Some ways to continue your education include:

1. Reading: There's a wealth of knowledge in books, financial news sites, and investment blogs. Read widely and critically.

2. Attending Seminars and Webinars: Many financial institutions and trading educators offer seminars and webinars on various trading topics.

3. Joining Trading Communities: Online forums and social media groups can be great places to connect with other traders, share ideas, and learn from each other's experiences.

4. Listening to Podcasts: Podcasts are an excellent way to learn about investing and trading while on the go. There are numerous podcasts available that cover a wide range of topics, from beginner-friendly explanations of basic concepts to in-depth discussions of advanced strategies.

5. Analyzing Your Own Trades: Every trade, whether successful or not, is an opportunity to learn. Analyze your decision-making process, identify what worked and what didn't, and look for ways to improve.

6. Staying Curious: Always be on the lookout for new ideas, strategies, and perspectives. Be open to challenging your own assumptions and learning from those with different viewpoints.

Remember, the market is a humbling place. No matter how much you learn, there will always be more to discover. Embrace the journey and enjoy the process of continuous growth.

Putting It All Together

When Nas rapped, "Be havin' dreams that I'm a gangsta, drinkin' Moëts, holdin' TEC's Makin' sure the cash came correct, then I stepped Investments in stock, sewin' up the blocks to sell rocks." It encapsulated the essence of the NY State of Mind mentality – it's about being strategic, seizing opportunities, and using your street smarts to get ahead with your legitimate business ventures without having to get involved with illicit activities. Just like a savvy investor in the stock market, a hustler on the streets of New York must be able to read people and situations, anticipate moves, and adapt to changing circumstances to survive and thrive.

In essence, Nas's lyric serves as a metaphor for the hustle and grind that characterizes the NY State of Mind, and how the skills and mindset one develops on the streets can be translated into the world of business and investing. It's about being shrewd, adaptable, and always staying one step ahead of the game, whether you're navigating the cutthroat world of finance or the dangerous streets of New York City.

Stock trading is a complex and multifaceted endeavor, requiring a blend of technical knowledge, strategic thinking, emotional discipline, and continuous learning. Like navigating the bustling streets of New York City, it demands alertness, adaptability, and a certain boldness of spirit.

But for those willing to put in the work and approach the markets with a "NY State of Mind" – a mindset of resilience, street smarts, and relentless pursuit of excellence – the rewards can be significant. With the right tools, mindset, and risk management strategies, stock trading can be a pathway to financial freedom and generational wealth.

As you embark on your own trading journey, remember the lessons of the market masters who came before you. Embrace the challenges, learn from your mistakes, and never stop growing. The market is always evolving, and so must you.

So put on your trading hat, fire up your charts, and get ready to take on the market, one trade at a time. The world of stock trading awaits, and with the right mindset, there's no limit to how far you can go. Welcome to the NYSE state of mind.

CHAPTER 2

LIFE'S A B**CH - RISK MANAGEMENT AND DIVERSIFICATION

"Load up the mic and bust one, cuss while I pus from, my skull, 'cause it's pain in my brain vein, money maintain, don't go against the grain, simple and plain."

Nas's story is not just one of a legendary rapper, but also of a savvy entrepreneur and investor who has navigated the high-stakes world of business with the same dexterity he brings to his rhymes.

Nas's journey from the streets of Queensbridge to the top of the music industry was not without its risks. In the early days of his career, Nas had to make bold moves to get his voice heard. His debut album, Illmatic, was a groundbreaking work that redefined the sound of East Coast hip-hop, but it was also a significant financial gamble. Nas invested his own money into the production of the album, betting on himself and his artistic vision.

This willingness to take calculated risks has been a hallmark of Nas's career, both in music and in business. After the success of Illmatic, Nas could have easily rested on his laurels, but instead, he continued to push himself creatively. He experimented with different sounds and styles, collaborating with a wide range of artists and producers. Some of these moves were more successful than others, but Nas always seemed to approach his career with a long-term perspective.

In many ways, Nas's approach to his music career mirrors the principles of effective risk management in investing. He diversified his creative portfolio, spreading his bets across different styles and collaborations. He was willing to take risks, but he also had a keen understanding of his own strengths and limitations. He knew when to double down on a winning formula, and when to cut his losses and move on.

But Nas's risk management strategies really came to the fore when he began to expand his business interests beyond music. In 2013 when he founded QVP, the firm's investment philosophy was rooted in the same principles that have guided Nas's music career: a willingness to take calculated risks, a focus on long-term growth, and a commitment to supporting visionary entrepreneurs.

One of QVP' most notable investments was in Ring, the smart doorbell company that was acquired by Amazon in 2018 for over $1 billion. Nas and his team recognized the potential of Ring early on, when it was still a fledgling startup. They saw the risk, but they also saw the enormous upside potential. By getting in on the ground floor, they were able to reap significant rewards when the company was acquired.

But Nas hasn't just focused on tech startups. He's also diversified his investment portfolio across a range of industries. He's invested in media companies like Mass Appeal and Genius, fashion brands like HSTRY, and even a cricket team in the Caribbean Premier League. This diversification strategy helps to mitigate risk, ensuring that Nas's financial fortune isn't tied to the success of any one venture.

Of course, not all of Nas's investments have been successful. He's had his share of misses along with his hits. But what sets Nas apart is his ability to learn from his mistakes and adapt his strategy accordingly. He doesn't let the fear of failure hold him back from taking risks, but he also doesn't let his ego cloud his judgment when it's time to pivot or cut his losses.

There's a lesson here for all investors. Building a successful investment portfolio is not about avoiding risk altogether, but rather about managing it effectively. It's about having the courage to take calculated bets, but also the humility to admit when you've made a mistake. It's about diversifying your holdings across a range of asset classes and industries, but also knowing when to concentrate your bets on a high-conviction opportunity.

Nas's journey also highlights the importance of patience and long-term thinking in investing. Just as he didn't expect Illmatic to make him an overnight success, Nas doesn't expect every investment to yield immediate returns. He's willing to ride out the ups and downs of the market, keeping his eye on the big picture.

This long-term mindset is especially important when it comes to startup investing, which is notoriously risky. The vast majority of startups fail, and even the successful ones can take years to generate significant returns. But for investors like Nas who are willing to play the long game, the potential rewards can be enormous.

Of course, not everyone has the financial resources or risk tolerance to invest in startups like Nas. But the principles of risk management and diversification apply to all investors, regardless of their level of wealth or expertise. Whether you're investing in stocks, bonds, real estate, or your own business, the key is to spread your bets, stay informed, and be willing to adapt your strategy as circumstances change.

Nas's story is a reminder that success in investing, as in life, is not about avoiding risk altogether, but about learning to manage it effectively. It's about having the courage to bet on yourself and your vision, but also the wisdom to know when to hedge your bets and diversify your holdings. It's about staying focused on the long game, even in the face of short-term setbacks and challenges.

In the end, balancing risk in your investment portfolio is not just a financial strategy, but a life philosophy. It's about embracing the uncertainty and volatility of the world, while still maintaining a sense of direction and purpose. It's about being willing to take chances, but also knowing when to play it safe. It's about learning from your mistakes, but not letting them define you.

Even Nas's music career had its share of controversy:

1. 2Pac: After 2Pac misinterpreted lines from Nas's album It Was Written as a diss towards him, he attacked Nas on his track "Against All Odds." The two later reconciled before 2Pac's untimely death.

2. Jay-Z: Initially friends, Nas and Jay-Z's relationship soured over the years, leading to a highly publicized feud. The two traded disses on songs like "Takeover" and "Ether," with Nas's "Ether" being widely regarded

as the decisive blow. The feud was officially squashed in 2005 when they performed together on stage.

3. Cam'ron: The feud began when Nas called Cam'ron's album "wack" on a radio show. Cam'ron responded with a freestyle diss, and the two continued to trade insults on various songs and mixtapes. They eventually reconciled in 2014.

4. Young Jeezy: Young Jeezy took offense to Nas's song "Hip Hop Is Dead," which blamed Southern hip hop for the genre's decline. Jeezy claimed Nas had "no street credibility," but later took back his disses, and the two collaborated on the hit single "My President."

5. Lijadu Sisters: Nas sampled the Lijadu Sisters' song "Life's Gone Down Low" on his mixtape without obtaining clearance or giving credit. The Nigerian twin sisters expressed their disappointment but acknowledged that Nas's use of their work showed they had created something of value.

6. Bill O'Reilly and Virginia Tech controversy: When Nas was set to perform at a Virginia Tech memorial concert, political commentator Bill O'Reilly criticized the decision, citing Nas's "violent" lyrics. Nas called O'Reilly a "chump" during the concert and later accused him of twisting facts for show ratings.

7. Doja Cat: In his song "Ultra Black," Nas described himself as "the opposite of Doja Cat," referencing accusations of her participating in racist conversations online. The response to the lyric was mixed, with some defending Nas and others resurfacing allegations of his past behavior. Nas later clarified that the line was not meant as a diss.

These various controversies and feuds throughout Nas's career highlight the importance of risk management in the world of hip-hop and entertainment. Just as investors must navigate the ups and downs of the stock market and make calculated decisions to mitigate potential losses, artists like Nas must carefully manage the risks associated with their public image, relationships, and creative choices. From the fallout of his feud with Jay-Z to the backlash over his sampling of the Lijadu Sisters' work, Nas has had to employ strategic thinking and adaptability to protect his reputation and maintain his success in the face of challenges. These experiences underscore the idea that, whether in the realm of music or investing, effective risk management is essential for long-term growth and resilience.

Nas's journey from Queensbridge to Wall Street is a testament to the power of this philosophy. Through his music and his business ventures, he's shown that with the right mindset and approach, it's possible to navigate even the riskiest waters and emerge stronger on the other side. As investors, we can all learn from his example, applying the principles of risk management and diversification to our own portfolios and our own lives.

Life may indeed be a b**ch sometimes, full of twists and turns and unexpected challenges. But with the right strategy and the right mindset, we can all learn to ride the waves of uncertainty and emerge victorious on the other side. That's the lesson of Nas's journey, and it's one that every investor can take to heart.

In the high-stakes world of investing, risk is an inescapable reality. Just as life can throw unexpected curveballs, the market can take sudden turns, leaving even the most seasoned investors reeling. But while risk may be a necessary part of the game, it doesn't have to be a deal-breaker. With the right strategies and mindset, it's possible to navigate the ups and downs of the market and come out on top. And one of the most powerful tools in the risk management arsenal? Diversification.

At its core, diversification is about spreading your bets. It's the investment equivalent of not putting all your eggs in one basket. By allocating your assets across a range of different securities, sectors, and asset classes, you can minimize the impact of any single investment's performance on your overall portfolio.

Think of it like this: imagine you're a rapper with a hot new single. If you put all your money and marketing muscle behind that one track, you might see some serious returns if it blows up. But what if it doesn't? What if the audience doesn't connect with it, or a scandal derails its momentum? Suddenly, you're left with nothing to fall back on.

Now, imagine instead that you spread your resources across a full album, with a diverse array of styles and collaborators. Even if one track underperforms, you've got others to pick up the slack. And if one really takes off, it can lift the whole project to new heights. That's the power of diversification.

But diversification isn't just about mitigating downside risk. It's also about positioning yourself to seize opportunities wherever they arise. By having a finger in multiple pies, you're better equipped to ride the waves of the market, capitalizing on growth in different sectors and asset classes as they emerge.

Of course, diversification isn't a magic bullet. It can't eliminate risk entirely, and it's not a substitute for due diligence and careful research.

But when used strategically, as part of a comprehensive risk management plan, it can be a game-changer.

So how do you go about building a diversified portfolio? Let's dive in.

Asset Allocation

The first step in diversifying your portfolio is to think about asset allocation. This refers to the way you split your investment capital across different asset classes, such as stocks, bonds, cash, real estate, and commodities.

Each of these asset classes has its own risk and return profile. Stocks, for example, have historically delivered higher returns over the long term, but they also come with higher volatility and risk of short-term losses. Bonds, on the other hand, tend to be less volatile and provide a steadier stream of income, but their returns are generally lower.

The key is to find a balance that aligns with your investment goals, risk tolerance, and time horizon. A younger investor with a longer time horizon and higher risk tolerance might allocate a larger portion of their portfolio to stocks, while an investor nearing retirement might shift more assets into bonds and cash to preserve capital.

One common approach is the 60/40 portfolio, which allocates 60% to stocks and 40% to bonds. This provides exposure to the growth potential of stocks while the bond allocation helps to smooth out the ride. However, this is just a starting point, and the right mix will depend on your individual circumstances.

It's also important to remember that asset allocation isn't a set-it-and-forget-it proposition. As your goals and circumstances change over time, you may need to adjust your allocation to stay on track. This is where the concept of rebalancing comes in - periodically resetting your portfolio back to its target allocation to maintain your intended risk level.

Diversification Within Asset Classes

While asset allocation is the foundation of a diversified portfolio, it's not the whole story. Within each asset class, there are further opportunities to diversify.

Let's take a closer look at diversification within the stock portion of your portfolio. When most people think of investing in stocks, they think of buying individual company shares. And while this can be a viable approach, it also comes with significant company-specific risk. If you put all your money into a single company, your fortunes are tied to the performance and fate of that one entity.

A more diversified approach is to invest in a broad range of companies across different sectors and industries. This way, you're not overly exposed to any one company or sector. If energy stocks are taking a hit due to falling oil prices, for example, your holdings in healthcare or technology might help offset those losses.

One way to achieve this broad market exposure is through mutual funds or exchange-traded funds (ETFs). These investment vehicles pool money from many investors to buy a basket of securities, providing instant diversification. An S&P 500 index fund, for example, would give you exposure to 500 of the largest US companies across a range of sectors.

But diversification doesn't stop at sector and industry. You can also diversify across geography (domestic vs international stocks), market capitalization (large-cap, mid-cap, small-cap stocks), and investment style (growth vs value stocks). Each of these dimensions offers potential for risk reduction and return enhancement.

On the bond side, diversification opportunities include varying maturities (short-term, intermediate-term, long-term), credit qualities (government, corporate, high-yield), and geographies (domestic, international, emerging markets).

The point is, within each slice of your asset allocation pie, there are further ways to slice and dice, spreading your bets and optimizing your risk/return profile.

The Role of Alternative Investments

For some investors, particularly those with larger portfolios, traditional stock and bond diversification may not be enough. This is where alternative investments come into play.

Alternative investments are assets that fall outside the traditional categories of stocks, bonds, and cash. They can include tangible assets like real estate, commodities, and precious metals, as well as financial contracts like options, futures, and hedge funds.

The appeal of alternative investments is that they often have low correlations with traditional assets, meaning they don't necessarily move in tandem with the stock or bond markets. This can provide an additional layer of diversification, helping to smooth out overall portfolio returns.

Real estate, for example, can offer a steady stream of rental income and the potential for capital appreciation, while also serving as a hedge against inflation. Commodities like gold are often seen as a safe haven in times of market turbulence or economic uncertainty.

However, alternative investments also come with their own set of risks and considerations. They can be less liquid (harder to buy and sell quickly), more volatile, and more complex than traditional investments. They may also require higher minimum investments and come with higher fees.

As with any investment, it's crucial to do your due diligence and understand what you're getting into before allocating funds to alternative investments. And as with traditional assets, diversification within alternative categories is key to managing risk.

Behavioral Aspects of Diversification

While the technical aspects of diversification are important, it's also crucial to consider the behavioral and psychological factors at play. Investing is an emotional game, and our own biases and impulses can often lead us astray.

One common pitfall is over-concentration in familiar assets. Many investors tend to gravitate towards companies or industries they know and understand, leading to portfolios that are heavily weighted in a particular sector or geography. Familiarity bias can also lead investors to overinvest in their employer's stock, tying their financial well-being to the fate of a single company.

Another behavioral trap is chasing performance - jumping on the bandwagon of the latest hot stock or sector, regardless of fundamentals or valuation. This can lead to buying high and selling low, the opposite of a sound investment strategy.

Diversification serves as a check against these behavioral biases. By committing to a broadly diversified portfolio, you're forced to look beyond your comfort zone and consider a wider range of opportunities. You're also less likely to get swept up in the hype of any single investment, as its impact on your overall portfolio is muted.

But diversification itself can also be emotionally challenging. It means accepting that not every investment will be a winner, and that you'll never fully capture the upside of any single stock or sector. It can be tempting to want to concentrate your bets on your highest-conviction ideas, especially in a bull market where it seems like every pick is a winner.

This is where having a disciplined, rules-based approach to diversification can be helpful. By setting clear asset allocation targets and rebalancing thresholds, you take the emotion out of the equation. You're not making ad hoc decisions based on the latest market moves, but rather sticking to a predetermined plan.

Of course, even the most disciplined investor is still human. There will always be the temptation to tinker, to make exceptions, to chase the hot hand. But by being aware of these behavioral pitfalls and putting guardrails in place, you can increase your chances of staying the course and reaping the long-term benefits of diversification.

Risk, Return, and the Efficient Frontier

At the heart of the diversification concept is the relationship between risk and return. In general, investments with higher potential returns come with higher risks, while safer investments offer lower returns. This is the fundamental trade-off that every investor must grapple with.

However, diversification offers a way to optimize this trade-off. By combining assets with different risk and return profiles, it's possible to create a portfolio that offers the highest expected return for a given level of risk, or the lowest risk for a given level of expected return.

This concept is captured by what's known as the efficient frontier. The efficient frontier is a graphical representation of the set of optimal portfolios that offer the highest expected return for each level of risk, or the lowest risk for each level of expected return.

Every possible combination of assets has a place on the risk/return spectrum, but the efficient frontier represents the best of the best - the portfolios that are optimally diversified to provide the most attractive risk/return trade-off.

Of course, the efficient frontier is a theoretical construct, and in practice, it's impossible to know precisely where it lies. But the principle remains: by carefully selecting and combining assets, it's possible to build a portfolio that's optimized for your specific risk tolerance and return objectives.

This is where the art and science of portfolio construction comes into play. Using tools like mean-variance optimization and Monte Carlo simulation, investment professionals can model different portfolio combinations and stress-test them under various market scenarios. The goal is to identify the asset mix that offers the best chance of meeting the investor's goals while staying within their risk comfort zone.

But it's important to remember that even an optimally diversified portfolio is not a guarantee against loss. Diversification is about managing risk, not eliminating it entirely. In times of broad market downturns, like the global financial crisis of 2008-2009, even well-diversified portfolios can suffer significant losses.

The key is to have a long-term perspective and to stay disciplined in your approach. By consistently rebalancing to your target allocations and resisting the urge to make dramatic shifts based on short-term market moves, you give yourself the best chance of weathering the storms and emerging successful on the other side.

The Limits of Diversification

While diversification is a powerful tool, it's not a panacea. There are limits to what diversification can achieve, and it's important to have realistic expectations.

One limitation is that diversification can only go so far in mitigating systematic risk, also known as market risk. This is the risk that affects the entire market, as opposed to any single company or sector. Events like natural disasters, geopolitical shocks, or broad economic downturns can cause the whole market to decline, dragging even a diversified portfolio down with it.

In these cases, the benefits of diversification are muted, as assets become more correlated and move in tandem. This is why it's important to have other risk management tools in your arsenal, such as tactical asset allocation, hedging strategies, or even holding a portion of your portfolio in cash or other safe-haven assets.

Another limitation is that diversification, taken to an extreme, can actually be counterproductive. Over-diversification, or "diworsification," can occur when you add so many assets to your portfolio that you dilute your returns without meaningfully reducing risk.

This can happen when you invest in too many overlapping or highly correlated assets, or when you spread your money across so many investments that none of them have a significant impact on your overall returns. The key is to strike a balance, ensuring you're diversified enough to manage risk, but not so much that you're sacrificing return potential.

It's also worth noting that diversification isn't free. Building and maintaining a diversified portfolio can come with costs, such as transaction fees, mutual fund expenses, and the time and effort required to research and monitor multiple investments. These costs can eat into your returns, so it's important to be mindful of them and to choose low-cost, efficient investment vehicles where possible.

Finally, it's crucial to remember that diversification is not a substitute for due diligence. No matter how broadly you spread your investments, you still need to do your homework on the individual assets you're buying. Diversification can help mitigate company-specific risk, but it can't protect you from the consequences of investing in a fundamentally unsound or overvalued security.

Putting It All Together

When Nas rapped, "Load up the mic and bust one, cuss while I pus from, my skull, 'cause it's pain in my brain vein, money maintain, don't go against the grain, simple and plain." He was drawing a parallel between the high-stakes world of street life and the equally challenging realm of financial management.

Let's break it down:

"Load up the mic and bust one, cuss while I pus from, my skull, 'cause it's pain in my brain vein"

Here, Nas is describing the intense pressure and mental strain that comes with navigating the harsh realities of the streets. He's "loading up the mic" to vent his frustrations and express the pain that's weighing on his mind.

"Money maintain, don't go against the grain, simple and plain"

In this line, Nas is offering a piece of advice that applies to both street life and financial management: stick to what you know, and don't take unnecessary risks. "Money maintain" suggests that the goal is to preserve and grow your wealth, while "don't go against the grain" is a warning against deviating from proven strategies or venturing into unfamiliar territory.

Nas's advice to "don't go against the grain" aligns with the concept of risk management in investing. Just as it's risky to stray from established practices in the street life, investors should be cautious about deviating from their chosen investment strategies or chasing after unproven trends. Sticking to a well-defined plan and avoiding impulsive decisions can help mitigate potential losses and ensure long-term financial stability.

Moreover, the idea of "money maintain" relates to the principle of diversification in investing. By spreading your investments across a range of assets and sectors, you can minimize the impact of any single loss and maintain a more stable financial foundation. This is similar to how, in the street life, having multiple streams of income or resources can provide a buffer against unexpected setbacks or challenges.

In essence, Nas's lyric serves as a reminder that, whether you're navigating the treacherous landscape of the streets or the complex world of finance, success depends on calculated risk-taking, adherence to proven strategies, and a commitment to long-term stability. By managing risk and diversifying your resources, you can weather the ups and downs of any environment and come out ahead in the end.

Crafting a well-diversified portfolio is a complex task that requires careful consideration of your goals, risk tolerance, and investment horizon. It involves making strategic decisions about asset allocation, selecting investments that complement each other, and regularly monitoring and rebalancing your holdings.

For many investors, particularly those just starting out, the process can seem daunting. This is where working with a financial professional can be helpful. An experienced advisor can help you navigate the complexities of diversification, tailoring a portfolio strategy to your unique needs and circumstances.

However, even if you're working with an advisor, it's important to educate yourself and stay engaged in the process. Ultimately, it's your money and your future, and you need to feel comfortable with and understand the investment decisions being made on your behalf.

One helpful framework for thinking about diversification is the core-satellite approach. In this model, the core of your portfolio is made up of broad-based, low-cost index funds or ETFs that provide wide market exposure. These core holdings are then supplemented with smaller allocations to more specialized, actively managed funds or individual securities that offer the potential for higher returns or specific diversification benefits.

For example, your core might consist of a total US stock market index fund, a total international stock index fund, and a broad-based bond fund. Your satellite holdings might include a real estate investment trust (REIT), a small-cap value fund, and an emerging markets bond fund.

The beauty of this approach is that it combines the efficiency and risk control of indexing with the flexibility and return potential of active management. It also allows you to adjust your allocations over time as your needs and circumstances change, without having to overhaul your entire portfolio.

Of course, this is just one approach among many. The key is to find a diversification strategy that works for you, one that balances your need for growth with your tolerance for risk, and that you can stick with over the long haul.

Because ultimately, successful investing is about consistency and discipline. It's about having a plan and sticking to it, even when the market is throwing curveballs. And that's where diversification really shines. By spreading your bets and controlling your risk, you give yourself the best chance of staying the course and achieving your long-term financial goals.

Life may indeed be a b**ch, full of twists and turns and unexpected challenges. But with a well-diversified portfolio in your corner, you'll be better equipped to roll with the punches and come out swinging. So take the time to understand the principles of diversification, to build a strategy that works for you, and to stay disciplined in your approach. Your future self will thank you.

CHAPTER 3

THE WORLD IS YOURS - IDENTIFYING INVESTMENT OPPORTUNITIES

"I'm out for dead presidents to represent me."

One of Nas's most notable investments in the media industry was his involvement in the revival of Mass Appeal magazine. Founded in 1996 as a graffiti fanzine, Mass Appeal had grown to encompass a wide range of pop culture topics, including hip-hop music, video games, cars, and movies. The magazine was known for its coverage of young artists and performers who contributed to and shaped contemporary hip-hop culture.

In 2013, Nas saw an opportunity to breathe new life into the Mass Appeal brand. He invested an undisclosed six-figure sum into the magazine, serving as the publication's associate publisher. Nas was joined in this venture by creative firm Decon and White Owl Capital Partners, an early-stage investment firm with business interests in technology, media, and energy located in North America, Europe, and China.

Nas's decision to invest in Mass Appeal was a strategic move that aligned with his deep understanding of hip-hop culture and his keen eye for identifying promising opportunities in the media landscape. As a veteran of the music industry and a highly respected figure in the hip-hop community, Nas recognized the potential of Mass Appeal to once again become a leading voice in the culture.

By investing in Mass Appeal, Nas was able to leverage his influence and network to attract top talent and collaborators to the magazine. His involvement also helped to bring a fresh perspective to the publication, ensuring that it remained relevant and engaging for a new generation of readers and fans.

Moreover, Nas's investment in Mass Appeal demonstrated his ability to spot a unique opportunity in a crowded media market. He recognized that there was still a strong demand for authentic, high-quality content that spoke directly to hip-hop culture and its diverse fan base. By partnering with Decon and White Owl Capital Partners, Nas was able to access the resources and expertise needed to scale the Mass Appeal brand and expand its reach across multiple platforms, including digital media, film, television, and music.

Nas's decision to invest in Mass Appeal magazine showcased his business acumen and his deep understanding of the power of media to shape culture and influence society. Through this investment, he not only helped to revive an iconic brand but also positioned himself as a visionary entrepreneur and cultural tastemaker in the world of hip-hop and beyond.

The ability to identify and capitalize on promising opportunities is what separates the winners from the losers. Just as Nas had to have his finger on the pulse of the streets to craft his groundbreaking rhymes, then later use those same instincts in business, successful investors must be attuned to the rhythms of the market, always on the lookout for the next big thing.

But with countless stocks to choose from and a constant barrage of information to sift through, how do you know where to focus your attention? How do you separate the true gems from the fool's gold? In this chapter, we'll dive deep into the art and science of researching and selecting stocks, drawing on the lessons of Nas's own journey from street poet to savvy investor.

The Power of Observation

The first step in identifying investment opportunities is simply to open your eyes and ears to the world around you. Nas didn't become one of the greatest rappers of all time by locking himself in a studio and shutting out the world. He drew inspiration from the streets, from the stories and struggles of the people he grew up with. He had a keen eye for detail and a gift for translating the raw materials of life into powerful, poetic narratives.

As an investor, you need to cultivate a similar sense of observation and curiosity. Pay attention to the products and services you use every day, the brands you encounter, and the trends you see emerging. When you notice something that catches your eye or piques your interest, don't just let it pass by. Dig deeper. Ask questions. Follow the trail.

This is how some of the most successful investors in history have made their fortunes. Peter Lynch, the legendary manager of the Magellan Fund at Fidelity Investments, was famous for his "invest in what you know" philosophy. He encouraged investors to look for investment ideas in their everyday lives, to pay attention to the companies they patronized and the products they used.

Lynch's approach was based on the simple but powerful idea that if a company's products or services are resonating with you, chances are they're resonating with others as well. And if a company is delivering value to its customers and gaining market share, it's likely to be a good investment.

Of course, just because you like a company's products doesn't mean it's automatically a good investment. There are many other factors to consider, which we'll get into later in this chapter. But the point is that by keeping your eyes and ears open to the world around you, you can start to generate a steady stream of potential investment ideas.

This is something that Nas has done throughout his career, both in music and in business. He's always been attuned to the spirit of the times, to the cultural currents that are shaping the world. When he first started investing in tech startups through QVP, he wasn't just chasing the latest fad. He was betting on the future, on the ideas and entrepreneurs that he believed had the potential to change the game.

Fundamental Analysis: The Foundation of Stock Selection

Once you've identified a company that piques your interest, the next step is to dig deeper into its fundamentals. This is where the real work of stock selection begins.

Fundamental analysis is the process of evaluating a company's financial health, business model, competitive position, and growth prospects to determine its intrinsic value. The goal is to identify companies that are undervalued by the market, that have strong fundamentals but are trading at a discount to their true worth.

There are many different aspects of a company to consider when conducting fundamental analysis, but some of the key factors include:

1. Financial Statements: A company's financial statements are like a window into its soul. They provide a detailed picture of its revenues, expenses, profits, assets, liabilities, and cash flows. By scrutinizing a company's income statement, balance sheet, and cash flow statement, you can get a sense of its financial health and performance over time.

Some key metrics to look at include:

- Revenue Growth: Is the company's revenue growing year over year? If so, at what rate? Steady, consistent revenue growth is a sign of a healthy business.

- Profitability: Is the company profitable? Look at metrics like gross margin, operating margin, and net margin to see how much of each dollar of revenue the company is able to convert into profits.

- Debt: How much debt does the company have relative to its assets and earnings? A highly leveraged company may be riskier than one with a cleaner balance sheet.

- Cash Flow: Is the company generating positive cash flow from its operations? Free cash flow (cash flow from operations minus capital expenditures) is a particularly important metric, as it represents the cash a company has available to invest in growth, pay dividends, or reduce debt.

2. Business Model: A company's business model is the engine that drives its financial performance. It encompasses everything from the products or services it offers to the way it makes money to the competitive dynamics of its industry.

Some key questions to ask when evaluating a company's business model include:

- What is the company's value proposition? What unique benefits does it offer to its customers?

- How does the company make money? Is it a one-time sale model or a recurring revenue model?

- What are the company's major costs? How scalable is the business?

- Who are the company's customers? Are they diversified or concentrated?

- What is the company's competitive position in its industry? Does it have a sustainable competitive advantage?

3. Management: A company is only as good as the people running it. When evaluating a potential investment, it's crucial to assess the quality and track record of the management team.

Some things to look for in a management team include:

- Experience: Does the team have a proven track record of success in the industry?

- Vision: Does the team have a clear, compelling vision for the future of the company?

- Integrity: Does the team have a reputation for honesty and transparency?

- Alignment: Are the interests of the management team aligned with those of shareholders?

4. Valuation: Finally, once you've assessed a company's fundamentals, you need to consider its valuation. Even a great company can be a bad investment if you overpay for it.

There are many different valuation metrics and models that investors use, but some of the most common include:

- Price-to-Earnings (P/E) Ratio: This is the price of a company's stock divided by its earnings per share. It gives you a sense of how much you're paying for each dollar of the company's earnings.

- Price-to-Sales (P/S) Ratio: This is the price of a company's stock divided by its revenue per share. It's useful for valuing companies that are not yet profitable.

- Discounted Cash Flow (DCF) Model: This is a more sophisticated valuation technique that involves estimating a company's future cash flows and discounting them back to the present at an appropriate rate.

The goal of valuation is not to find the "perfect" price for a stock, but rather to determine whether it is trading at a significant discount to its intrinsic value. If you can buy a dollar's worth of value for 50 cents, you're setting yourself up for strong potential returns.

The principles of valuation and finding undervalued opportunities are at the core of Nas's approach to investing. Rather than chasing the latest hot stock or trying to time the market, he focuses on identifying companies with strong fundamentals and long-term growth potential, and then investing in them when they're trading at a discount to their intrinsic value. This patient, value-oriented approach has served him well over the years, as evidenced by some of his most successful investments.

Let's take a closer look at a few case studies from Nas's investment portfolio that illustrate this approach in action:

1. Coinbase

One of Nas's most successful investments to date has been in Coinbase, the cryptocurrency exchange platform. Through QVP, Nas got in on the ground floor of Coinbase back in 2013, when the company was still relatively unknown.

At the time, the idea of a digital currency exchange was still novel and risky. But Nas and his team saw the potential in Coinbase's business model and the growing demand for cryptocurrency trading. They believed in the vision of the company's founders and saw an opportunity to get in early on what could be a transformative technology.

Their bet paid off in a big way. When Coinbase went public in April 2021, it was valued at over $85 billion. Nas's stake in the company was estimated to be worth between $34 million and $173 million, depending on the exact number of shares he owned.

The Coinbase investment showcases several key aspects of Nas's approach to investing. He was willing to take a risk on a novel, unproven concept, but he did so based on a careful analysis of the market opportunity and the strength of the company's leadership team. He had the patience to hold onto his investment for the long term, even as the cryptocurrency market went through its ups and downs. And he had the vision to see the potential for transformative growth in a nascent industry.

2. Ring

Another notable investment in Nas's portfolio is Ring, the smart doorbell company that was acquired by Amazon in 2018 for over $1 billion.

Nas and his team at QVP invested in Ring in 2014, back when it was still a startup known as DoorBot. At the time, the idea of a Wi-Fi-enabled doorbell with a built-in camera was still relatively novel. But Nas saw the potential in the product and believed in the vision of the company's founder, Jamie Siminoff.

Over the next few years, Ring grew rapidly, fueled by strong demand for its products and several rounds of additional funding. By the time Amazon came knocking in 2018, Ring had become a household name and a leader in the smart home security space.

For Nas, the Ring investment was a perfect example of the "invest in what you believe in" philosophy that we mentioned earlier. He saw a product that he himself would use and that he believed could make people's lives better. He backed a founder with a strong vision and a track record of execution. And he had the patience to hold onto his investment as the company scaled, knowing that the real payoff would come down the road.

The Ring acquisition was a major win for Nas and his team, generating a significant return on their initial investment. But more than that, it was a validation of Nas's approach to investing - backing strong founders, believing in transformative products, and having the patience to let those bets play out over time.

3. Pluto TV

Pluto TV is a streaming television service that offers free access to over 250 channels of content, ranging from news and sports to movies and classic TV. Nas and his team at QVP invested in Pluto TV in 2014, seeing the potential for a free, ad-supported streaming platform to disrupt the traditional cable TV model.

Over the next few years, Pluto TV grew rapidly, expanding its content offerings and user base. In 2019, the company was acquired by Viacom (now ViacomCBS) for $340 million, generating a significant return for Nas and his fellow investors.

The Pluto TV investment showcases Nas's ability to identify and capitalize on emerging trends in the media and technology space. He saw the potential for a free streaming service to capture a large audience in an increasingly cord-cutting world. And he had the foresight to back a company that was well-positioned to execute on that vision, with a strong leadership team and a differentiated content strategy.

The Pluto TV acquisition also highlights the importance of strategic partnerships in Nas's investment approach. By aligning with a major media company like Viacom, Pluto TV was able to accelerate its growth and reach a wider audience. And for Nas and his team, the acquisition provided a valuable exit opportunity and a strong return on their initial investment.

These case studies illustrate some of the key principles that have guided Nas's success as an investor:

1. Identify emerging trends and markets with strong growth potential.

2. Back strong founders and leadership teams with a clear vision and a track record of execution.

3. Invest in products and services that solve real problems and make people's lives better.

4. Take a long-term view and have the patience to let investments play out over time.

5. Look for strategic partnerships and exit opportunities that can accelerate growth and generate strong returns.

Of course, not every investment in Nas's portfolio has been a home run. Like any investor, he's had his share of misses along with his hits. But by staying true to these core principles and learning from his mistakes, he's been able to build a diverse and successful portfolio that spans multiple industries and stages of growth.

As aspiring investors looking to follow in Nas's footsteps, we can learn a lot from these case studies. We can learn to think strategically about emerging trends and markets, to back strong founders and products, and to take a long-term view on our investments. We can learn to be patient and disciplined, to stay the course even when the road gets bumpy. And we can learn to always be on the lookout for new opportunities, new partnerships, and new ways to create value.

Just like Nas himself, we may not hit a home run with every investment we make. But by staying true to our principles and learning from our mistakes, we can build a portfolio that generates strong returns and makes a real impact on the world. That's the power of the Nas approach to investing - and it's a power that we can all tap into if we're willing to put in the work and stay the course.

Putting It All Together

I'm out for presidents to represent me (say what?)
I'm out for presidents to represent me (say what?)
I'm out for dead presidents to represent me!!!!!!

In this lyric from his iconic song "The World Is Yours," Nas is using a clever play on words to express his ambition and his approach to identifying investment opportunities.

"I'm out for dead presidents to represent me"

Here, "dead presidents" is a slang term for money, referring to the images of deceased U.S. presidents that appear on American currency. By saying he's "out for dead presidents," Nas is declaring his intention to acquire wealth and success.

However, the line can also be interpreted on a deeper level. When Nas says he wants dead presidents to "represent" him, he's suggesting that he wants his wealth and success to speak for itself. He's not interested in empty hype or superficial recognition; instead, he wants his accomplishments and his financial status to be a testament to his skill, his hustle, and his strategic thinking.

Nas's lyric embodies the mindset of a savvy investor who is always on the lookout for lucrative opportunities. Just as Nas is "out for dead presidents," a successful investor is constantly seeking ways to grow their wealth and expand their portfolio.

But the key to identifying profitable investments is not just about chasing money for its own sake. Like Nas, a wise investor wants their wealth to "represent" them – to reflect their values, their expertise, and their ability to make smart, calculated decisions.

This means doing thorough research, staying attuned to market trends and emerging industries, and being willing to take calculated risks when the right opportunity presents itself. It also means having a clear understanding of one's own strengths and weaknesses and being able to distinguish between hype and genuine potential.

Nas's investment in Mass Appeal is a prime example of this approach in action. By identifying an undervalued asset in the media industry and leveraging his own knowledge and network to help it grow, Nas was able to create significant value for himself and his partners. His wealth and success in this venture "represent" his strategic thinking, his industry expertise, and his ability to spot untapped potential in a crowded market.

In essence, Nas's lyric encapsulates the mindset of a true entrepreneur and investor – one who is constantly hustling to create value, but who also understands that real wealth and success come from making smart, purposeful decisions that reflect one's skills and values. It's a reminder that, in both music and business, the key to achieving your goals is to stay focused on the long game and to always be on the lookout for opportunities that will help you level up and build a legacy that lasts.

This may seem like science with predictable outcomes, but it is also an art. Fundamental analysis is a powerful tool for identifying promising investment opportunities, but it's not the whole story. To be a successful investor, you also need to have a keen understanding of market dynamics, risk management, and your own investment goals and constraints.

One way to think about it is like crafting a great rap song. Just as Nas carefully selects his words and phrases to create a powerful, cohesive verse, investors need to carefully select stocks that fit together into a diversified, resilient portfolio.

This means considering factors like:

- Sector Diversification: Spreading your investments across different sectors of the economy, such as technology, healthcare, finance, and consumer goods.

- Geographic Diversification: Investing in companies that operate in different regions of the world, to mitigate the risk of any one country or region.

- Market Capitalization: Balancing investments in large, established companies with smaller, faster-growing firms.

- Risk Tolerance: Choosing investments that align with your personal risk tolerance and investment timeline.

Just like in the studio, creating a great investment portfolio is an iterative process. You can't expect to get it perfect on the first take. You need to be willing to tweak and refine your approach over time, learning from your successes and mistakes.

This is something that Nas has done throughout his career. He's never been afraid to experiment with new sounds and styles, to push himself out of his comfort zone. But he's also never lost sight of his core strengths and values. He's stayed true to his roots while constantly evolving and adapting to the changing landscape.

As an investor, you need to bring that same spirit of creativity and adaptability to your approach. The world of investing is constantly changing, with new companies, technologies, and economic forces emerging all the time. To stay ahead of the curve, you need to be willing to keep learning, keep experimenting, and keep refining your strategies.

Common Pitfalls and How to Avoid Them

Of course, even the most disciplined and diligent investors can fall prey to common pitfalls and biases. Here are a few to watch out for:

1. Confirmation Bias: This is the tendency to seek out information that confirms your existing beliefs and ignore information that contradicts them. As an investor, it's crucial to be objective and open-minded, to consider all the evidence before making a decision.

2. Herd Mentality: It's easy to get caught up in the latest market fads and trends, to follow the crowd instead of thinking for yourself. But just because everyone else is buying a stock doesn't mean it's a good investment. Stick to your own analysis and convictions.

3. Overconfidence: Many investors overestimate their ability to predict the future and underestimate the role of luck and randomness in the markets. Stay humble and remember that even the best investors are wrong sometimes.

4. Short-Term Thinking: It's tempting to focus on short-term price movements and try to time the market, but this is a recipe for stress and subpar returns. Instead, take a long-term view and focus on the underlying fundamentals of the companies you invest in.

The Role of Patience and Discipline

Perhaps the most important lesson that Nas's journey can teach us about investing is the power of patience and discipline. Just as Nas didn't achieve overnight success with Illmatic, building a successful investment portfolio takes time and consistent effort.

It's easy to get caught up in the daily ups and downs of the market, to let your emotions drive your decisions. But the best investors are able to tune out the noise and stay focused on their long-term goals. They have the discipline to stick to their strategies even when the going gets tough, and the patience to let their investments compound over time.

This is something that Nas has embodied throughout his career. He's had his share of setbacks and challenges, but he's never let them define him. He's always kept his eye on the bigger picture, on the legacy he wants to leave behind.

As an investor, you need to bring that same sense of purpose and perspective to your approach. You need to be willing to ride out the short-term volatility in pursuit of long-term gains. You need to have the discipline to stick to your principles and the patience to let your investments bear fruit.

And just as importantly, you need to have faith in yourself and your ability to navigate the ever-changing landscape of the markets. Like Nas, you need to believe that the world is yours for the taking, that with hard work, smart strategies, and a little bit of luck, you can achieve your financial dreams.

The Importance of Continuous Learning

Of course, no one becomes a great investor overnight. Like any craft, it takes years of practice, study, and experimentation to master the art of stock selection.

That's why continuous learning is so crucial. Just as Nas has never stopped pushing himself to grow and evolve as an artist, successful investors never stop learning and adapting to new market realities.

This means staying up to date on the latest news and trends in the industries you invest in, reading financial statements and analyst reports, attending conferences and webinars, and seeking out the wisdom of more experienced investors.

It also means being willing to learn from your mistakes. Every investor makes bad calls sometimes, but the key is to use those experiences as opportunities for growth and improvement. By analyzing what went wrong and adjusting your approach accordingly, you can become a smarter, more resilient investor over time.

The Role of Mentorship and Collaboration

One of the most powerful ways to accelerate your learning and growth as an investor is to seek out mentorship and collaboration from those who have already achieved success in the field.

This is something that Nas has done throughout his career, from his early days learning from legendary producers like Large Professor and DJ Premier, to his later collaborations with artists like Damian Marley and Hit-Boy.

As an investor, you can benefit from the same kind of mentorship and collaboration. This might mean joining an investment club or online community, attending events and conferences, or even seeking out a personal mentor who can guide you on your journey.

The key is to surround yourself with people who share your passion for investing, who can challenge you to think in new ways and push you to be your best self. By learning from and collaborating with others, you can accelerate your own growth and achieve your investment goals faster.

The Power of Perseverance

Finally, perhaps the most important lesson that Nas's journey can teach us about investing is the power of perseverance. Just as Nas has faced countless obstacles and setbacks on his path to success, every investor will face challenges and adversity at some point.

The key is to never give up, to keep pushing forward even when the odds seem stacked against you. Like Nas, you need to have an unshakeable belief in yourself and your ability to overcome any obstacle.

This means staying focused on your long-term goals, even when the short-term outlook is uncertain. It means being willing to take calculated risks and make bold moves when the time is right. And it means having the resilience to bounce back from losses and keep moving forward.

Investing is not for the faint of heart. It requires a special kind of mental toughness and emotional fortitude. But for those who are willing to put in the work and stay the course, the rewards can be truly life-changing.

So as you embark on your own journey to identify and capitalize on investment opportunities, remember the lessons of Nas's remarkable career. Stay curious and observant, always on the lookout for new ideas and insights. Do your homework and analyze companies from every angle before making a move. Stay patient and disciplined, focused on the long game rather than short-term fluctuations.

Surround yourself with mentors and collaborators who can help you grow and evolve as an investor. And above all, never lose faith in yourself and your ability to achieve your dreams. The world of investing may be complex and ever-changing, but with the right mindset and approach, the world truly is yours for the taking.

As Nas himself might say, the stock market is like the streets - it's not always pretty, but for those who know how to navigate it, it can be a path to unimaginable wealth and success. So keep your head up, your eyes open, and your mind sharp. The opportunities are out there, waiting for those bold enough to seize them. It's time to make your move.

PART II: THE STARTUP SYMPHONY - VENTURING INTO STARTUPS

CHAPTER 4

HALFTIME - EVALUATING STARTUPS LIKE A PRO

"I used to hustle, now all I do is relax and strive."

Nas's investment in Mass Appeal magazine was a strategic move that not only revived the influential publication but also laid the foundation for the creation of Mass Appeal Records. Founded in 2014, Mass Appeal Records is an American independent record label that operates as the music division of the Mass Appeal Media Group. The label was launched by Nas in collaboration with Peter Bittenbender, Co-founder and CEO of Decon, a New York-based advertising agency and record label.

This partnership between Nas and Bittenbender showcased Nas's entrepreneurial spirit and his keen ability to identify and nurture talent in the music industry. By leveraging the brand recognition and cultural influence of Mass Appeal magazine, Nas was able to create a platform for up-and-coming artists to showcase their skills and reach a wider audience.

As a startup, Mass Appeal Records quickly established itself as a force to be reckoned with in the music industry. The label boasts an impressive roster of artists, including DJ Shadow, Mannie Fresh, Dave East, Fashawn, Black Milk, and Keyon Harrold, among others. These artists represent a diverse range of styles and backgrounds, reflecting Nas's commitment to supporting innovative and groundbreaking music across multiple genres.

Nas's investment in Mass Appeal magazine and the subsequent creation of Mass Appeal Records demonstrate his ability to identify promising opportunities in the media and music industries. By combining his deep understanding of hip-hop culture with his business acumen and industry connections, Nas has been able to build a thriving media empire that encompasses publishing, music, film, television, and digital content.

Moreover, the success of Mass Appeal Records as a startup is a testament to Nas's vision and leadership. By providing a platform for emerging talent and fostering a creative environment that values authenticity and innovation, Nas has helped to shape the future of the music industry and cement his legacy as a cultural icon and business leader.

Mass Appeal Records itself can be viewed as a startup that has successfully navigated the competitive landscape of the music industry. The label's success can be attributed to its ability to identify and develop talented artists, as well as its strategic partnerships and collaborations. For example, the label's release of Run the Jewels' critically acclaimed album "Run the Jewels 2" in 2014 demonstrates its ability to recognize and support groundbreaking artists. Additionally, Mass Appeal Records' joint venture with Pulse Music Group in 2017 and its partnership with Universal Music Group in 2018 showcase the label's strategic growth and expansion.

In many ways, the success of Mass Appeal Records mirrors the key factors that Nas looks for when evaluating startups as an investor. Just as he seeks out companies with strong founding teams, innovative products, and significant market potential, Nas has built Mass Appeal Records by identifying talented artists, supporting creative projects, and capitalizing on opportunities for growth and collaboration. As both a successful rapper and a savvy businessman, Nas has demonstrated his ability to translate his skills and instincts from the music industry to the world of startups and entrepreneurship.

So, what makes a startup investment-worthy? The ability to separate the winners from the losers is what sets the pros apart from the amateurs. Just as Nas had to have an ear for talent and potential when scouting new acts for his record label, successful startup investors must be able to identify the companies with the right mix of vision, execution, and market opportunity to turn a great idea into a thriving business.

But with countless startups vying for attention and funding, how do you know which ones are worth betting on? What are the key factors that distinguish a truly investment-worthy startup from the rest of the pack? In this chapter, we'll take a deep dive into the art and science of startup evaluation, drawing on the lessons and insights of Nas and other top investors who have made their mark in the world of venture capital.

The Founder Factor

When it comes to evaluating startups, there's no factor more important than the quality and vision of the founding team. A great idea is only as good as the people who are tasked with bringing it to life, and a startup's success or failure often hinges on the strength of its leadership.

As an investor, your job is to look beyond the pitch deck and the product demo to get a sense of who the founders are as people. What drives them?

What unique skills and experiences do they bring to the table? How do they handle adversity and setbacks?

One key quality to look for in a founding team is passion. Building a successful startup is a long and grueling journey, filled with countless obstacles and challenges. The founders who are most likely to succeed are the ones who are deeply passionate about their mission and vision, and who have the grit and determination to keep pushing forward even when the going gets tough.

Another important factor is expertise. The best founding teams are typically made up of individuals with deep knowledge and experience in the industry or market they're targeting. They have a clear understanding of the problem they're trying to solve and the customers they're trying to serve, and they bring a unique set of skills and insights to bear on the challenge.

Diversity is also key. Startups with diverse founding teams - in terms of background, expertise, and perspective - tend to be more resilient and adaptable than those with a more homogeneous makeup. They're better equipped to navigate the complex challenges of building and scaling a business, and they bring a wider range of ideas and approaches to the table.

Of course, evaluating founding teams is as much an art as a science. There's no simple formula or checklist that can tell you whether a particular team has what it takes to succeed. As an investor, you need to rely on your own judgment and intuition, honed through years of experience and observation.

One way to get a sense of a founding team's strengths and weaknesses is to spend time with them in person, either through formal pitch meetings or more casual interactions. Pay attention to how they communicate and collaborate with each other, how they respond to tough questions and feedback, and how they articulate their vision and strategy.

You can also look at their track record and background to get a sense of their capabilities and potential. Have they successfully built and scaled companies before? Do they have a strong network of advisors, mentors, and industry connections? Have they demonstrated the ability to attract and retain top talent?

Ultimately, backing the right founding team is as much about trust and relationship-building as it is about objective analysis. As an investor, you're not just betting on a company - you're betting on the people behind it. By taking the time to get to know the founders and understand what makes them tick, you can make more informed and confident decisions about where to place your bets.

Market Opportunity and Timing

Of course, even the strongest founding team can't succeed if they're targeting the wrong market or timing their entry poorly. That's why the next key factor to consider when evaluating startups is the size and growth potential of the market they're going after.

The best startups are typically those that are targeting large, rapidly-growing markets with significant unmet needs or pain points. These are the markets where there's room for multiple winners to emerge, and where even a small slice of the pie can translate into significant revenues and profits.

One way to assess market potential is to look at the total addressable market (TAM) - the total amount of revenue that could be generated if the company captured 100% of its target market. While no company ever achieves full market penetration, the TAM provides a useful benchmark for understanding the overall size and scope of the opportunity.

Another important factor to consider is timing. The most successful startups are often those that enter the market at just the right moment, when the stars are aligning in terms of technology, consumer behavior, and regulatory environment. Think of companies like Uber and Airbnb, which emerged at a time when smartphones, digital payments, and the sharing economy were all hitting critical mass.

As an investor, your job is to look beyond the current state of the market to anticipate where it's headed in the future. This requires a deep understanding of the underlying trends and forces that are shaping consumer behavior, technological innovation, and business models.

One way to stay on top of these trends is to immerse yourself in the industry or sector you're focused on. Attend conferences and trade shows, read industry publications and analyst reports, and network with other investors and entrepreneurs who are active in the space.

You can also look for signs of market validation and traction, such as early customer adoption, partnerships with established players, or positive media coverage. These can all be indicators that a startup is onto something big and that the market is ripe for disruption.

Ultimately, timing the market is as much a matter of luck as it is skill. Even the most promising startups can be derailed by unexpected events or shifts in the competitive landscape. As an investor, your job is to make informed bets based on the best available information, while also being prepared to pivot or cut your losses if the market moves in an unexpected direction.

Product and Technology

Another key factor to consider when evaluating startups is the strength and differentiation of their product or technology. In today's hyper-competitive startup landscape, it's not enough to simply have a good idea - you need to be able to execute on that idea better than anyone else.

When assessing a startup's product or technology, there are a few key questions to ask:

1. Is it solving a real problem or meeting a genuine need in the market? The best products are those that address a clear pain point or unmet need for customers, rather than simply being a solution in search of a problem.

2. Is it differentiated from existing solutions in the market? To succeed, a startup needs to be able to offer something that's truly unique and valuable, whether it's a new technology, a better user experience, or a more efficient business model.

3. Is it scalable and defensible? A great product is only valuable if it can be delivered at scale and if it can be protected from imitation or competition. Look for startups that have a clear path to scalability and that have built moats around their technology or business model, such as patents, proprietary algorithms, or network effects.

4. Is it well-designed and user-friendly? In today's digital age, the user experience is often just as important as the underlying technology. Look

for startups that have invested in design and usability, and that have a clear understanding of their target customers and their needs.

Of course, evaluating a startup's product or technology is not always straightforward, especially for investors who may not have deep technical expertise. That's why it's important to rely on a network of experts and advisors who can provide informed opinions and insights.

One way to get a sense of a startup's product or technology is to try it out for yourself, if possible. Sign up for a demo or a free trial, kick the tires, and see how it compares to other solutions in the market. Pay attention to the little details - the user interface, the onboarding process, the customer support - as these can all be indicators of the overall quality and thoughtfulness of the product.

You can also look for signs of customer traction and engagement, such as user reviews, case studies, or metrics around retention and usage. These can all be indicators that the product is resonating with its target audience and that there's real demand for what the startup is offering.

Ultimately, backing a startup with a great product or technology is about more than just betting on the idea itself - it's about betting on the team's ability to execute on that idea and to continually innovate and improve over time. By looking beyond the surface-level features and functionality to understand the deeper value proposition and competitive advantage, you can make more informed decisions about which startups are worth your investment.

Business Model and Financials

Of course, no matter how great the founding team, market opportunity, or product may be, a startup ultimately needs to have a viable business model and strong financial fundamentals to succeed in the long run. As an investor, it's critical to dig into the details of how a startup plans to make money and to assess the sustainability and scalability of its revenue streams.

One key factor to consider is the startup's unit economics - the revenue and costs associated with each individual customer or transaction. A startup with strong unit economics is one that can generate a profit on each sale, even at a relatively small scale. This is a good indicator of the underlying health and viability of the business model.

Another important factor is the startup's growth trajectory and burn rate. Most startups will be unprofitable in their early stages as they invest heavily in product development, customer acquisition, and scaling their operations. However, it's important to understand how quickly the startup is growing its revenue and customer base, and how efficiently it is using its capital to fuel that growth.

As an investor, you'll want to look for startups that have a clear path to profitability and that are managing their cash carefully to extend their runway as long as possible. This may involve tough choices around hiring, marketing spend, and other investments, but it's critical for ensuring the long-term sustainability of the business.

You'll also want to pay close attention to the startup's fundraising history and capitalization table. How much money has the company raised to date, and from whom? What is the current valuation and ownership structure? Are there any red flags or potential conflicts of interest among the investors or board members?

These are all important questions to ask when evaluating a startup's financial health and risk profile. You'll want to make sure that you're investing on terms that are fair and reasonable, and that you have a clear understanding of your rights and obligations as an investor.

It's also worth noting that not all startups will have a traditional revenue model or path to profitability. Some may be focused on building a large user base or ecosystem first, with the goal of monetizing later through advertising, subscriptions, or other means. Others may be pursuing a "blitzscaling" strategy of rapid growth and market domination, even at the expense of short-term profits.

As an investor, it's important to be clear-eyed about the risks and trade-offs involved in these different approaches, and to make sure that you're comfortable with the startup's strategic direction and timeline for achieving its goals.

Competitive Landscape

No startup exists in a vacuum, and understanding the competitive landscape is critical for assessing a company's chances of success. Who are the other players in the market, and how do they stack up in terms of product, technology, and market share? What are the barriers to entry, and how defensible is the startup's position?

One way to assess the competitive landscape is to conduct a thorough market analysis, looking at factors such as market size, growth rate, and segmentation. This can help you understand the overall dynamics of the industry and identify potential opportunities or threats.

You'll also want to look at the specific competitors in the startup's space, both direct and indirect. What are their strengths and weaknesses, and how do they compare to the startup in terms of product, pricing, and target customers? Are there any emerging trends or technologies that could disrupt the status quo?

It's also worth considering the potential for new entrants or substitutes. Even if a startup has a strong position in its current market, there's always the risk that a new player could come in and shake things up. This is especially true in fast-moving, technology-driven industries where the barriers to entry may be lower than in traditional industries.

As an investor, you'll want to look for startups that have a clear and compelling value proposition that sets them apart from the competition. This could be a unique technology or product feature, a more efficient business model, or a deeper understanding of customer needs and preferences.

You'll also want to pay attention to the startup's go-to-market strategy and its ability to execute on that strategy. How does the company plan to acquire customers and drive adoption of its product or service? What channels and tactics will it use to reach its target audience? And how will it measure and optimize its marketing and sales efforts over time?

Ultimately, the goal is to invest in startups that have a sustainable competitive advantage and a clear path to market leadership. By understanding the competitive landscape and the startup's place within it, you can make more informed decisions about which companies are worth betting on for the long haul.

Due Diligence and Risk Assessment

Of course, no matter how promising a startup may seem on paper, there are always risks and uncertainties involved in early-stage investing. That's why thorough due diligence and risk assessment are critical components of the startup evaluation process.

Due diligence typically involves a deep dive into the company's legal, financial, and operational details, as well as its technology and intellectual property. This may include reviewing contracts and agreements, analyzing financial statements and projections, and conducting background checks on key personnel.

The goal of due diligence is to uncover any potential red flags or risk factors that could impact the startup's success or the investor's return on investment. These could include issues such as pending lawsuits, regulatory compliance problems, or key employee departures.

As an investor, it's important to have a clear and systematic approach to due diligence, and to work with experienced legal and financial advisors who can help you navigate the complexities of the process. You'll want to make sure that you have access to all the relevant information and documentation, and that you take the time to thoroughly review and assess the risks and opportunities.

In addition to legal and financial due diligence, it's also important to consider other types of risk that may be specific to the startup or its industry. For example, a startup that relies heavily on user-generated content or social media may face higher risks around content moderation, privacy, and security. A startup in a heavily regulated industry such as healthcare or finance may face additional compliance burdens and regulatory scrutiny.

As an investor, you'll want to work closely with the startup's leadership team to understand and mitigate these risks as much as possible. This may involve implementing robust policies and procedures, investing in compliance and security measures, or seeking out strategic partnerships or advisors with relevant expertise.

Ultimately, the goal of due diligence and risk assessment is not to eliminate risk entirely - that's impossible in the world of early-stage investing. Rather, it's about understanding and managing risk in a way that aligns with your investment goals and risk tolerance. By taking a proactive and systematic approach to evaluating and mitigating risk, you can increase your chances of success and minimize the potential for costly mistakes or oversights.

The Art of the Deal

Of course, even the most thorough evaluation process is only the beginning when it comes to startup investing. Once you've identified a company that you believe in and that meets your investment criteria, the real work begins: negotiating the terms of the deal and structuring the investment in a way that aligns with your goals and risk tolerance.

There are many different factors to consider when structuring a startup investment, including the size and timing of the investment, the valuation and equity stake, the liquidation preferences and other investor rights, and the governance and decision-making processes.

As an investor, you'll want to work closely with your legal and financial advisors to craft a deal that balances your interests with those of the startup and its other investors. This may involve tough negotiations and trade-offs, but it's critical for ensuring that everyone is aligned and that the investment has the best possible chance of success.

One key consideration is the stage of the startup and the level of risk involved. Early-stage investments tend to be higher risk but also higher reward, while later-stage investments may offer more stability but lower potential returns. As an investor, you'll want to think carefully about your own risk tolerance and investment goals, and structure your portfolio accordingly.

Another important factor is the level of involvement and control that you want to have as an investor. Some investors prefer to take a hands-off approach, providing capital but leaving the day-to-day operations and decision-making to the startup's leadership team. Others may want to take a more active role, serving on the board of directors or providing strategic guidance and support.

There's no one-size-fits-all approach to startup investing, and the right structure will depend on a wide range of factors specific to the company, the market, and the investors involved. The key is to be clear about your own goals and expectations upfront, and to work collaboratively with the startup and other investors to find a structure that works for everyone.

Of course, even the best-laid plans can go awry, and startup investing is inherently risky and uncertain. That's why it's important to have a clear and well-defined exit strategy in place from the outset, whether that's through an acquisition, an IPO, or another liquidity event.

As an investor, you'll want to work closely with the startup's leadership team to understand their long-term vision and plans for the company, and to ensure that everyone is aligned around the potential exit opportunities and timelines. You'll also want to have a clear understanding of your own liquidity needs and preferences, and structure your investment accordingly.

Evaluating startups is both an art and a science, requiring a unique blend of analytical rigor, strategic vision, and gut instinct. It's a high-stakes game where the potential for outsized rewards is matched only by the risk of significant losses, and where the difference between success and failure can often come down to small details and intangibles.

As an investor, the key is to approach the process with a clear and well-defined set of criteria, a deep understanding of the market and competitive landscape, and a willingness to do the hard work of due diligence and risk assessment

So, how can you use Nas's approach to startups to further your start up investing journey? Nas has developed a unique set of criteria for assessing the viability and growth potential of early-stage companies. His approach can be broken down into several key components:

1. Founder and Team: Nas places a strong emphasis on the quality and expertise of the founding team. He looks for passionate, knowledgeable, and driven entrepreneurs who have a clear vision for their company and the ability to execute on their ideas. Nas also values diversity in the team, recognizing that a range of perspectives and skill sets can contribute to a startup's success.

2. Market Potential: When evaluating a startup, Nas assesses the size and growth potential of the target market. He looks for companies that are addressing a significant problem or need, with a clear value proposition

and a large addressable market. Nas also considers the competitive landscape and the startup's ability to differentiate itself from existing players.

3. Product and Technology: Nas pays close attention to the quality and innovation of a startup's product or technology. He looks for companies that are developing unique, scalable solutions with a strong value proposition for customers. Nas also assesses the startup's intellectual property and its ability to stay ahead of the curve in terms of technology and user experience.

4. Traction and Metrics: Nas evaluates a startup's traction and key performance indicators to gauge its potential for growth and success. He looks at metrics such as user acquisition, retention, revenue growth, and unit economics to assess the company's current performance and future potential.

5. Strategic Partnerships: Nas values startups that have established strategic partnerships or have the potential to form meaningful collaborations. He recognizes the importance of leveraging relationships and networks to accelerate growth, gain market share, and create value for all stakeholders involved.

6. Alignment with Personal Values: As an investor, Nas also considers how a startup aligns with his personal values and interests. He has a particular focus on companies that are driving positive social impact, promoting diversity and inclusion, and creating opportunities for underserved communities.

Pulling It All Together

In "Halftime" when Nas rapped, "I used to hustle, now all I do is relax and strive" he was reflecting on his journey from the streets to the boardroom, and the mindset shift that comes with transitioning from a hustler to a successful entrepreneur. Let's break it down and tie it to the concept of evaluating startups like a pro.

"I used to hustle, now all I do is relax and strive"

Here, Nas is contrasting his past life as a hustler on the streets with his current reality as a successful businessman. The word "hustle" implies a constant grind, a need to always be on the move and looking for the next opportunity. But now that he's achieved a level of success and financial stability, he can "relax" – not in the sense of being lazy or complacent, but in the sense of having the freedom and security to focus on his larger goals and aspirations.

The word "strive" is key here. Even though Nas is no longer hustling in the literal sense, he's still driven by a desire to achieve more, to push himself and his ventures to new heights. The difference is that now, he can pursue those goals from a position of strength and stability, rather than a place of desperation or survival.

Nas's lyric also speaks to the mindset and approach of a seasoned startup investor. Just like Nas has evolved from a street hustler to a savvy businessman, the best startup investors are those who have learned to "relax and strive" – to use their experience and expertise to make calculated, strategic decisions, rather than chasing after every shiny opportunity that comes their way.

When evaluating startups, a pro knows how to cut through the noise and focus on the fundamentals. They look for strong founding teams with the right mix of skills and experience, large and growing market opportunities, and differentiated products or services with clear competitive advantages. They also know how to assess a startup's traction, scalability, and potential for long-term growth, and how to structure deals that align the interests of founders, investors, and other stakeholders.

But just like Nas, the best startup investors also know that success is about more than just the numbers. They strive to build strong, collaborative relationships with the founders and teams they back, providing guidance, support, and resources to help them navigate the challenges of building and scaling a business. They also know how to balance the need for quick, decisive action with the patience and perspective required to build lasting value over time.

In essence, Nas's lyric encapsulates the mindset of a true startup investor – one who has the experience and expertise to make smart, calculated decisions, but also the passion and drive to keep pushing forward and striving for more. It's a reminder that, in both the streets and the startup world, success comes not just from hustling hard, but from knowing when and how to "relax and strive" towards your larger goals and vision.

Once you are relaxing and striving It also means that you did your due diligence and have trust in the company and team you are invested in. In the world of startup investing, the ability to identify and back promising companies is a skill that sets the most successful investors apart from the rest. As we've seen throughout this chapter, evaluating startups is a multifaceted process that requires a keen eye for talent, a deep understanding of market dynamics, and a strategic approach to building a diversified portfolio.

Nas's journey as both a musician and an investor offers valuable insights into what makes a startup investment-worthy. His approach to evaluating startups is grounded in his own experiences as an artist and entrepreneur, and reflects his unique perspective on what it takes to succeed in a competitive and constantly evolving landscape.

At the core of Nas's investment philosophy is a focus on the founding team. Just as he surrounded himself with talented producers, musicians, and collaborators throughout his music career, Nas looks for startup founders who are passionate, knowledgeable, and committed to their vision. He recognizes that a strong team with diverse skill sets and perspectives is essential for navigating the challenges and opportunities of the startup world.

Nas also places a strong emphasis on market potential and product innovation. He looks for companies that are addressing significant problems or needs, with a clear value proposition and a large addressable market. He assesses the competitive landscape and looks for startups that have the potential to disrupt existing players or create entirely new categories.

In addition to these fundamental factors, Nas also considers a range of other criteria when evaluating startups. He looks at traction and key performance indicators to gauge a company's current performance and future potential. He values strategic partnerships and collaborations that can accelerate growth and create value for all stakeholders involved. And he considers how a startup aligns with his personal values and interests, with a particular focus on companies that are driving positive social impact and creating opportunities for underserved communities.

Ultimately, what sets Nas apart as an investor is his ability to combine his instincts, experience, and strategic thinking into a holistic approach to startup evaluation. He doesn't just look at a company's financial metrics or market potential in isolation, but rather considers how all of these factors work together to create a compelling investment opportunity.

For aspiring investors and entrepreneurs, Nas's approach offers a valuable framework for thinking about what makes a startup investment-worthy. By focusing on the quality of the founding team, the size and growth potential of the market, the innovation and scalability of the product, and the company's traction and strategic partnerships, investors can increase their chances of identifying and backing the most promising startups.

Of course, no investment is without risk, and even the most promising startups can face significant challenges and setbacks along the way. That's why Nas's approach also emphasizes the importance of building a diversified portfolio and being prepared for the ups and downs of the startup world.

As we've seen throughout this chapter, Nas's own journey as an investor has been marked by both successes and failures. He's had his share of hits, like his early investments in Coinbase and Dropbox, as well as some misses along the way. But through it all, he's remained committed to his vision and his belief in the power of entrepreneurship to drive positive change in the world.

In many ways, Nas's approach to startup investing is a reflection of his own journey as an artist and entrepreneur. He's always been willing to take risks, to push boundaries, and to bet on himself and his ideas. He's also been committed to lifting up others along the way, using his platform and his resources to create opportunities for the next generation of leaders and innovators.

As the startup world continues to evolve and new challenges and opportunities emerge, Nas's approach to evaluating startups offers a roadmap for investors and entrepreneurs alike. By staying true to his principles, constantly learning and adapting, and always keeping an eye on the bigger picture, Nas has established himself as one of the most influential and successful investors in the game.

So whether you're a seasoned investor looking to refine your approach, or an entrepreneur just starting out on your journey, take a page from Nas's playbook. Focus on building a strong team, identifying big market opportunities, and creating innovative products that solve real problems. Surround yourself with smart, passionate people who share your vision and your values. And always be willing to take risks, learn from your mistakes, and keep pushing forward, no matter what obstacles come your way.

In the end, that's what makes a startup investment-worthy: a combination of talent, vision, innovation, and perseverance. And that's what sets the most successful investors and entrepreneurs apart from the rest. As Nas has shown us time and again, when you have those ingredients in place, the sky's the limit. So let's keep dreaming big, taking risks, and building the future, one investment at a time.

CHAPTER 5

ONE LOVE - BUILDING RELATIONSHIPS IN THE STARTUP WORLD

"Word to mother, I heard him frontin' And he be pumpin' on your block Your man gave him your Glock And now they run together — what up, son? Whatever."

Success is not just about having a great idea or a talented team. It's also about building strong relationships and leveraging the power of networks to open doors, gain insights, and accelerate growth. Just as Nas has built a legendary career in music through collaborations and partnerships, successful entrepreneurs and investors know that the key to thriving in the startup world is to cultivate a rich ecosystem of mentors, advisors, and allies.

Throughout Nas's illustrious career in the music industry,

He has cultivated relationships with a wide range of other music industry players, from record labels and distributors to producers and fellow artists. He has collaborated with some of the biggest names in hip-hop, including Jay-Z, Kanye West, and Kendrick Lamar, as well as with artists from other genres, such as Damian Marley and Amy Winehouse. These collaborations have not only produced some of the most memorable and influential tracks in hip-hop history but have also helped to bridge gaps between different musical communities and generations.

Nas's ability to build and maintain relationships in the music industry extends beyond just his creative collaborations. He has also been a savvy business partner, forming strategic alliances with brands like Hennessy and Fila to create unique marketing and promotional opportunities. He has also been a mentor and advisor to younger artists, using his platform and influence to help them navigate the challenges of the music industry and build sustainable careers.

Perhaps most importantly, Nas's relationship-building skills have been rooted in a deep sense of authenticity and respect for the culture and the communities that have shaped him as an artist and a person. Whether he's working with a longtime collaborator or a new up-and-coming talent, Nas approaches each interaction with a sense of humility, curiosity, and a genuine desire to create something meaningful and impactful.

In the cutthroat world of the music industry, where relationships can be fleeting and transactional, Nas's ability to cultivate genuine, long-lasting partnerships has been a key factor in his success and longevity. By prioritizing authenticity, creativity, and mutual respect in all of his collaborations and ventures, Nas has not only built a legendary career for himself but has also helped to create a more vibrant, inclusive, and innovative music community for generations to come.

In this chapter, we'll explore the art and science of networking and mentorship in the startup world, drawing on the experiences of Nas and other successful entrepreneurs and investors. We'll examine the different types of relationships that are critical for startup success, the strategies and tactics for building and nurturing those relationships, and the ways in which mentorship can accelerate learning and growth for both mentors and mentees.

The Power of Networks

At its core, the startup world is a network of people and ideas. It's a complex web of entrepreneurs, investors, advisors, customers, and partners, all working together to create value and drive innovation. And just like any network, the strength and resilience of the startup ecosystem depends on the quality and diversity of the connections within it.

For entrepreneurs, building a strong network is essential for accessing the resources, expertise, and opportunities needed to turn a great idea into a successful business. Whether it's finding the right investors, recruiting top talent, or partnering with key customers and suppliers, a well-developed network can open doors and create possibilities that would be impossible to access on one's own.

But building a network is not just about collecting business cards or adding connections on LinkedIn. It's about cultivating genuine relationships based on trust, respect, and mutual value creation. It's about taking the time to listen, learn, and understand the needs and goals of others, and finding ways to support and empower them in their own journeys.

One of the key principles of effective networking is the idea of "giving before you get." Instead of approaching networking with a transactional mindset, focused solely on what others can do for you, successful networkers prioritize creating value for others first. They look for ways to share their own knowledge, resources, and connections, without expecting anything in return. And in doing so, they build a reputation as generous, trustworthy, and valuable members of the community.

Another important aspect of networking is diversity and inclusion. In a world where innovation and creativity thrive on the exchange of different perspectives and ideas, it's critical to build networks that span across different industries, backgrounds, and experiences. By actively seeking out and engaging with people who are different from oneself, entrepreneurs and investors can tap into new sources of insight and opportunity, and build more resilient and adaptable businesses.

The Role of Mentorship

One of the most powerful ways to accelerate learning and growth in the startup world is through mentorship. Whether it's a seasoned entrepreneur sharing their hard-won wisdom with a first-time founder, or an investor providing guidance and support to a promising startup, mentorship is a critical driver of success in the fast-moving and uncertain world of entrepreneurship.

At its core, mentorship is about the transfer of knowledge, skills, and experience from one person to another. It's about providing guidance, support, and accountability to help mentees navigate the challenges and opportunities of starting and growing a business. And it's about creating a safe and trusting environment where mentees can take risks, make mistakes, and learn from their experiences.

But mentorship is not a one-way street. While mentees certainly benefit from the wisdom and expertise of their mentors, mentors also gain valuable insights and perspectives from their interactions with mentees. By engaging with the next generation of leaders and innovators, mentors stay connected to the cutting edge of their industries, and gain new ideas and approaches that can inform their own work and decision-making.

Effective mentorship requires a combination of skills and qualities, including empathy, active listening, constructive feedback, and a willingness to share one's own failures and vulnerabilities. Great mentors are not just experts in their fields, but also skilled communicators and relationship builders who can adapt their approach to the unique needs and learning styles of their mentees.

One of the key benefits of mentorship is that it can help entrepreneurs and investors avoid common pitfalls and mistakes. By learning from the experiences of those who have gone before them, mentees can shortcut their own learning curves and make more informed decisions about their businesses. Mentors can also provide valuable introductions and connections to key players in the startup ecosystem, helping mentees build their own networks and access new opportunities.

Another important aspect of mentorship is that it can provide a source of emotional support and encouragement during the inevitable ups and downs of startup life. Starting and growing a business is a rollercoaster ride of highs and lows, and having a trusted mentor to turn to for advice and perspective can be invaluable for maintaining motivation and resilience in the face of challenges.

Building Relationships with Investors

For entrepreneurs, one of the most critical relationships to build in the startup world is with investors. Whether it's angel investors, venture capitalists, or strategic partners, having the right investors on board can provide the capital, expertise, and connections needed to fuel growth and scale.

But building relationships with investors is not just about pitching and closing deals. It's about creating a foundation of trust, transparency, and alignment that can support a long-term partnership. Investors are not just looking for great ideas or impressive traction, but also for founders who they can trust to execute on their vision and create value for all stakeholders.

To build strong relationships with investors, entrepreneurs need to focus on a few key areas. First and foremost, they need to have a deep understanding of their business and market, and be able to articulate a compelling vision for the future. They need to be transparent about their challenges and opportunities, and be willing to engage in honest and open dialogue with investors about their progress and plans.

Entrepreneurs also need to be proactive in building relationships with investors, even before they are actively seeking funding. This can involve attending industry events and conferences, participating in startup accelerators and incubators, and actively seeking out introductions and referrals from trusted advisors and mentors.

When it comes time to pitch investors, entrepreneurs need to be prepared and professional. This means having a clear and concise pitch deck that highlights the key elements of the business, including the problem being solved, the target market, the competitive landscape, and the revenue model. It also means being able to answer tough questions and provide evidence to support key assumptions and projections.

But building relationships with investors is not just about the initial pitch and deal. It's also about maintaining open and regular communication throughout the life of the investment, and being responsive to investor needs and concerns. This can involve providing regular updates on key metrics and milestones, seeking input and guidance on strategic decisions, and being transparent about any challenges or setbacks that arise.

Networking and Relationship-Building Strategies

So how can entrepreneurs and investors build and nurture the relationships that are so critical for startup success? Here are a few key strategies and tactics to consider:

1. Attend industry events and conferences: These gatherings provide a great opportunity to meet and connect with other entrepreneurs, investors, and experts in your field. Come prepared with business cards and a clear elevator pitch, and be proactive in seeking out conversations and introductions.

2. Join startup communities and groups: Whether it's online forums, local meetups, or global networks like Entrepreneur's Organization or Young Presidents' Organization, being part of a community of like-minded entrepreneurs can provide valuable support, resources, and connections.

3. Seek out mentors and advisors: Look for experienced entrepreneurs, investors, or experts who have successfully navigated the challenges you

are facing, and reach out to them for guidance and advice. Be respectful of their time and expertise, and look for ways to provide value in return.

4. Offer your own expertise and resources: One of the best ways to build relationships is to be a valuable resource for others. Look for opportunities to share your own knowledge and connections, and be generous with your time and advice.

5. Follow up and stay in touch: Building relationships takes time and effort, and it's important to stay in touch even after the initial connection has been made. Follow up with a thank-you note or email, and look for ways to keep the conversation going over time.

6. Be authentic and genuine: At the end of the day, the most successful relationships are built on a foundation of trust and authenticity. Don't try to be someone you're not, or pretend to have all the answers. Be honest about your strengths and weaknesses, and look for ways to create genuine connections based on shared values and goals.

Case Studies and Examples

To bring these concepts to life, let's take a look at a few real-world examples of entrepreneurs and investors who have successfully built and leveraged relationships in the startup world.

One example is the story of Troy Carter, the founder and CEO of Atom Factory, a talent management and full-service film and television production company. Carter has built a reputation as one of the most influential figures in the music industry, having managed the careers of artists like Lady Gaga, John Legend, and Meghan Trainor. He has also been a successful investor, with early stakes in companies like Uber, Lyft, and Dropbox.

Carter's success in the music industry and the startup world has been largely due to his ability to build and maintain strong relationships. He has a reputation for being a compassionate and supportive manager, prioritizing the well-being and long-term success of his clients over short-term gains. He has also been intentional about building a diverse network of contacts across different industries, from tech and finance to media and entertainment.

Another example is the story of Jewel Burks Solomon, the co-founder and CEO of Partpic, a startup that uses computer vision technology to streamline the process of finding and ordering replacement parts for maintenance and repair. Solomon and her co-founder Jason Crain built Partpic from the ground up, leveraging their relationships with mentors, advisors, and investors to scale the company and attract top talent.

Solomon has been a vocal advocate for diversity and inclusion in the tech industry, using her platform to inspire and empower underrepresented founders and communities. She has been intentional about building a strong network of supportive peers and mentors, and has used her success with Partpic to pay it forward to the next generation of entrepreneurs.

Finally, let's look at the example of Nas himself, who has built a successful career as both a musician and an investor through the power of relationships and collaboration. From his early days working with producers and fellow artists in the studio, to his more recent investments in startups like Coinbase, Dropbox, and Casper, Nas has always prioritized building strong relationships based on trust, respect, and shared value creation.

As an investor, Nas has also been intentional about using his platform and resources to support and empower underrepresented founders and communities. Through QVP, Nas has invested in a range of startups and initiatives that are driving positive social and economic change, from education and healthcare to financial inclusion and social justice.

The Importance of Diversity and Inclusion

As mentioned earlier, one of the key principles of effective networking and relationship-building is diversity and inclusion. In a world where innovation and creativity thrive on the exchange of different perspectives and ideas, it's critical to build networks and teams that span across different backgrounds, experiences, and identities.

But diversity and inclusion are not just about checking boxes or meeting quotas. They are about creating a culture of belonging and empowerment, where everyone feels valued and supported in bringing their full selves to the table. And they are about recognizing and addressing the systemic barriers and biases that have historically excluded or marginalized certain groups from full participation in the startup ecosystem.

For entrepreneurs and investors, this means being intentional and proactive in seeking out and engaging with diverse talent and perspectives. It means creating inclusive environments and practices that support the success and advancement of underrepresented groups, such as women, people of color, LGBTQ+ individuals, and people with disabilities. And it means being willing to have uncomfortable conversations and take actionable steps to address inequities and create more equitable outcomes.

By prioritizing diversity and inclusion in their networking and relationship-building efforts, entrepreneurs and investors can not only tap into new sources of innovation and opportunity, but also create more resilient and adaptable businesses that reflect the full spectrum of human experience and potential.

Overcoming Challenges and Setbacks

Of course, building and maintaining relationships in the startup world is not always easy. Entrepreneurs and investors face a range of challenges and setbacks along the way, from misaligned expectations and communication breakdowns to personal and professional conflicts.

One common challenge is the power imbalance that can exist between entrepreneurs and investors, particularly in the early stages of a startup's journey. Entrepreneurs may feel pressure to accept unfavorable terms or compromise their vision in order to secure funding, while investors may be tempted to use their leverage to exert undue influence or control over the business.

To navigate these challenges, it's important for both entrepreneurs and investors to establish clear expectations and boundaries from the outset, and to communicate openly and honestly about their needs and concerns. This can involve setting up regular check-ins and progress reports, establishing clear metrics and milestones for success, and having difficult conversations about potential risks and trade-offs.

Another common challenge is the personal and emotional toll that startup life can take on founders and their teams. The high-pressure, fast-paced environment of the startup world can lead to burnout, stress, and mental health issues, particularly when compounded by the financial and personal sacrifices that many entrepreneurs make in pursuit of their dreams.

To mitigate these risks, it's important for entrepreneurs to prioritize self-care and work-life balance, and to build a strong support network of friends, family, and mentors who can provide emotional and practical support along the way. It's also important for investors to recognize and support the holistic well-being of their portfolio founders, and to provide resources and support for mental health and wellness.

Collaborations and Partnerships

In the startup world, collaborations and partnerships are essential for achieving scale, entering new markets, and creating value for all stakeholders. By joining forces with other companies, organizations, or individuals, startups can leverage complementary strengths, resources, and networks to achieve goals that would be impossible to reach alone.

There are many different types of collaborations and partnerships that startups can pursue, depending on their stage, sector, and goals. Some common examples include:

1. Strategic alliances: These are long-term partnerships between companies that share common goals and interests, and that work together to create mutual value. Strategic alliances can take many forms, from joint ventures and co-branding initiatives to shared research and development projects.

2. Channel partnerships: These are partnerships between companies that have complementary products or services, and that can cross-promote each other's offerings to their respective customer bases. Channel partnerships can help startups expand their reach and generate new revenue streams without having to build their own sales and marketing teams from scratch.

3. Ecosystem partnerships: These are partnerships between companies that are part of the same industry or ecosystem, and that work together to create shared standards, platforms, or infrastructures. Ecosystem partnerships can help startups tap into network effects and create more value for their users and customers.

4. Social impact partnerships: These are partnerships between startups and non-profit organizations, government agencies, or other stakeholders that are focused on creating positive social or environmental impact. Social impact partnerships can help startups align their business goals with broader societal needs, and create more sustainable and inclusive solutions.

To build successful collaborations and partnerships, startups need to be strategic and proactive in their approach. This means identifying potential partners that have shared values, complementary strengths, and aligned incentives, and reaching out to them with a clear value proposition and plan for collaboration.

It also means being transparent and communicative throughout the partnership process, and establishing clear roles, responsibilities, and metrics for success. Partnerships are not always easy, and they require ongoing effort and attention to maintain trust, alignment, and performance over time.

One key factor in successful partnerships is the ability to create win-win outcomes for all parties involved. This means looking beyond short-term transactional benefits and focusing on creating long-term value and impact for everyone. It also means being willing to compromise and adapt as needed, and to prioritize the needs and goals of the partnership over individual interests.

Another important factor is the ability to build strong personal relationships and trust with partners. Partnerships are ultimately about people working together towards a common goal, and the strength of those interpersonal connections can make all the difference in overcoming obstacles and achieving success.

Finally, successful partnerships require a willingness to learn and grow together, and to embrace the challenges and opportunities that come with collaboration. Partnerships can be a powerful source of innovation and value creation, but they also require a certain level of risk-taking and experimentation. By staying open to new ideas and approaches, and by learning from both successes and failures, startups can build more resilient and impactful partnerships over time.

Pulling It All Together

Building relationships in the startup world is a complex and multi-faceted endeavor, but one that is essential for achieving success and impact. Whether it's through networking, mentorship, investor relationships, or collaborations and partnerships, the ability to build and leverage strong human connections is what sets the most successful entrepreneurs and investors apart.

When Nas rapped, "Word to mother, I heard him frontin' And he be pumpin' on your block Your man gave him your Glock And now they run together — what up, son? Whatever."

from his song "One Love," Nas is telling a cautionary tale about the dangers of misplaced trust and the importance of building authentic, loyal relationships in the face of adversity.

"Word to mother, I heard him frontin' And he be pumpin' on your block Your man gave him your Glock And now they run together — what up, son? Whatever."

Here, Nas is describing a situation where someone's trusted friend or partner has betrayed them, joining forces with a rival or enemy who is now operating on their turf ("pumpin' on your block"). The fact that the friend gave the rival access to the person's weapon ("your Glock") suggests a deep level of betrayal and a complete disregard for loyalty and trust.

Nas's dismissive "whatever" at the end of the verse underscores the sense of disappointment and resignation that comes with being let down by someone you thought had your back. It's a reminder that not everyone who claims to be on your side is truly looking out for your best interests.

Just like in the street life Nas describes, the startup world is full of potential rivals, fair-weather friends, and people who are only looking out for themselves.

As an entrepreneur or investor, it's important to be discerning about the people you choose to work with and the partnerships you form. You need to be able to trust that the people in your corner are truly invested in your success and are willing to stick with you through the ups and downs of building a business.

This means taking the time to really get to know potential partners, investors, and employees, and looking for signs of genuine alignment and shared values. It means being willing to have difficult conversations and set clear expectations and boundaries upfront, rather than assuming that everyone is on the same page.

It also means being loyal and supportive to the people who have proven themselves to be trustworthy allies, even when the going gets tough. In the startup world, as in life, relationships are tested by adversity and challenges. The people who are still standing by your side when the chips are down are the ones who truly have your back.

Ultimately, Nas's lyric is a reminder that building authentic, loyal relationships is not always easy, but it's essential for navigating the complex, competitive landscape of the startup world. By being discerning, communicative, and committed to your allies, you can create a strong foundation of trust and support that will help you weather any storm and achieve your goals.

It's about quality over quantity, depth over breadth. As Nas puts it, "what up, son? Whatever." In other words, focus on the relationships that really matter, and don't waste your time or energy on those who don't have your best interests at heart. That's the key to building a strong, resilient network that will support you through the challenges and opportunities of startup life.

As we've seen throughout this chapter, building relationships requires a combination of skills, strategies, and mindsets. It requires a willingness to give before you get, to listen and learn from others, and to prioritize diversity and inclusion in all aspects of your work. It requires a commitment to authenticity, transparency, and trust, and a willingness to put in the time and effort to nurture and grow your relationships over time.

At the same time, building relationships in the startup world is not always easy. It can be challenging to navigate power imbalances, communication breakdowns, and personal and professional conflicts. It can be tempting to prioritize short-term gains over long-term value, or to focus on transactional exchanges rather than genuine human connections.

But as Nas and other successful entrepreneurs and investors have shown us, the power of relationships and collaboration is what drives real change and impact in the world. By prioritizing empathy, authenticity, and shared purpose in our relationship-building efforts, we can tap into the full potential of human creativity and innovation, and create businesses and initiatives that reflect the richness and complexity of the human experience.

So let us take inspiration from the concept of "one love," and build a startup ecosystem that is grounded in the principles of unity, diversity, and shared prosperity. Let us use our platforms and resources to empower and support each other, and to create a world that works for everyone. And let us remember that the true measure of our success is not just in the products we create or the profits we generate, but in the strength and resilience of the relationships we build along the way.

In the end, building relationships in the startup world is about more than just business strategy or personal growth. It's about the power of human connection to transform ourselves and the world around us. It's about the potential for shared purpose and impact, and the belief that together, we can achieve anything we set our minds to.

So let us go forth with open hearts and minds, ready to listen, learn, and grow together. Let us build a startup ecosystem that is grounded in the principles of one love, and that empowers us all to create a brighter, more just, and more abundant future together. And let us remember that the true measure of our success is not just in the products we create or the profits we generate, but in the strength and resilience of the relationships we build along the way.

CHAPTER 6

IT AIN'T HARD TO TELL - FROM STARTUP TO SUCCESS

"It ain't hard to tell, I excel, then prevail The mic is contacted, I attract clientele."

Chauncey Alexander Hollis Jr., better known as Hit-Boy, is a talented young producer who has made a significant impact in the music industry. Despite his relatively short career compared to veteran rapper Nas, Hit-Boy has managed to form an unlikely but highly successful partnership with the Queensbridge legend. Together, they have created six albums, one of which finally earned Nas a Grammy Award after 17 nominations.

Nas and Hit-Boy's incredible musical journey together is a perfect example of how a startup mentality can lead to remarkable success in the music industry. Their collaboration can be likened to a startup venture, where Nas, as the experienced entrepreneur, took a calculated risk by partnering with Hit-Boy, a young and talented producer, to create something innovative and groundbreaking.

Just as startups often face challenges and uncertainties, the idea of a veteran rapper like Nas working with a relatively new producer like Hit-Boy might have seemed unlikely at first. However, Nas's willingness to take a chance on Hit-Boy's creativity and fresh perspective mirrors the mindset of successful entrepreneurs who recognize the potential in emerging talent and ideas.

The success of their partnership can be measured not only by the critical acclaim their albums have received but also by the fact that Nas finally won his first Grammy Award after 17 nominations. This achievement is comparable to a startup reaching a significant milestone or securing a major investment, validating the hard work and risk-taking that went into the venture.

Moreover, Hit-Boy's ability to manifest his dreams and goals is a testament to the power of vision and determination in both the music industry and the startup world. By setting clear objectives and working tirelessly to achieve them, Hit-Boy has not only fulfilled his aspirations but also surpassed them, creating a lasting partnership with Nas that has yielded six albums and two trilogies in just three years.

The longevity and consistency of Nas and Hit-Boy's collaboration is reminiscent of a startup that has successfully navigated the challenges of growth and scaled its operations. Their ability to maintain a high level of quality and innovation across multiple projects is a rare feat in the music industry, much like a startup that manages to sustain its momentum and stay ahead of the curve in a competitive market.

Furthermore, Nas's openness to continuing his creative partnership with Hit-Boy shows a commitment to long-term growth and success, similar to how successful startups continue to evolve and adapt to new opportunities and challenges. By fostering a culture of collaboration, trust, and shared vision, Nas and Hit-Boy have built a strong foundation for enduring success, not unlike the values that underpin thriving startup teams.

In essence, the story of Nas and Hit-Boy's collaboration is a powerful example of how the principles of entrepreneurship and startup culture can be applied to the music industry. By embracing risk, recognizing talent, setting ambitious goals, and maintaining a focus on innovation and quality, they have created a successful partnership that has not only yielded impressive results but also serves as an inspiration for aspiring artists and entrepreneurs alike.

The journey from idea to success is never a straight line. It's a winding path filled with obstacles, setbacks, and pivots, where the difference between failure and success often comes down to the ability to adapt, persevere, and scale effectively. As Nas has shown us throughout his legendary career, the key to long-term success is not just about having talent or vision, but about having the right strategies and mindset to take your game to the next level.

In this chapter, we'll explore the art and science of scaling and growth in the startup world, drawing on the experiences of successful entrepreneurs, investors, and experts who have cracked the code on how to take a promising idea and turn it into a thriving, sustainable business. We'll examine the key stages of the startup journey, the common pitfalls and challenges that entrepreneurs face along the way, and the proven strategies and tactics for overcoming those obstacles and achieving exponential growth.

The Startup Journey

Before we dive into the specifics of scaling and growth, it's important to understand the typical trajectory that most startups follow on their path to success. While every startup is unique, there are some common stages and milestones that most companies go through as they evolve and mature.

1. Ideation and Validation

The first stage of the startup journey is all about coming up with a great idea and validating that there is a real market need and opportunity for it. This is where entrepreneurs do their initial research, talk to potential customers, and test their assumptions about the problem they're trying to solve and the solution they're proposing.

At this stage, the focus is on developing a clear value proposition, identifying the target market, and creating a minimum viable product (MVP) that can be used to test and refine the concept. This is also where entrepreneurs start to build their initial team, secure initial funding or investment, and lay the groundwork for the next stages of growth.

2. Early Traction and Product-Market Fit

Once the initial idea has been validated, the next stage is all about gaining early traction and achieving product-market fit. This is where startups start to see their first real customers, revenue, and growth, and where they begin to refine and optimize their product, business model, and go-to-market strategy based on real-world feedback and data.

At this stage, the focus is on building a scalable and repeatable sales and marketing engine, developing key partnerships and channels, and creating a strong brand and customer experience that can drive word-of-mouth and organic growth. This is also where startups start to bring on additional team members, build out their operations and infrastructure, and raise additional funding to fuel their growth.

3. Growth and Scaling

Once a startup has achieved product-market fit and started to gain significant traction, the next stage is all about accelerating growth and scaling the business to the next level. This is where startups start to see exponential growth in their customer base, revenue, and market share, and where they begin to face new challenges and opportunities as they expand into new markets, products, and geographies.

At this stage, the focus is on building a scalable and efficient organization that can support rapid growth, developing new products and services to expand the customer base and revenue streams, and creating a strong company culture and team that can attract and retain top talent. This is also where startups start to face increased competition, regulatory challenges, and other external factors that can impact their growth and success.

4. Maturity and Exit

The final stage of the startup journey is all about achieving maturity and planning for an eventual exit or liquidity event. This is where startups have established themselves as leaders in their market, with a strong brand, customer base, and financial position, and where they begin to think about their long-term strategic options and legacy.

At this stage, the focus is on optimizing the business for profitability and cash flow, exploring strategic partnerships, acquisitions, or IPOs, and ensuring a smooth transition for the team, customers, and stakeholders. This is also where startups start to think about their broader impact and legacy, and how they can use their success and platform to drive positive change in the world.

Of course, these stages are not always linear or predictable, and every startup will face its own unique challenges and opportunities along the way. But by understanding the typical trajectory and milestones of the startup journey, entrepreneurs can better prepare themselves for the road ahead and make more informed decisions about how to scale and grow their business.

Common Scaling Challenges and Pitfalls

While the startup journey is full of exciting opportunities and possibilities, it's also fraught with challenges and pitfalls that can derail even the most promising companies. Here are some of the most common scaling challenges that startups face, and some strategies for overcoming them:

1. Premature Scaling

One of the biggest mistakes that startups make is trying to scale too quickly before they have achieved product-market fit or built a solid foundation for growth. Premature scaling can lead to a host of problems, from burning through cash too quickly to losing focus on the core value proposition to creating a culture of chaos and burnout.

To avoid premature scaling, startups need to be disciplined and strategic about when and how they invest in growth. This means setting clear milestones and metrics for success, and only scaling up when those milestones have been achieved. It also means being realistic about the resources and capabilities needed to support growth, and not overextending the team or the business beyond its means.

2. Losing Focus on the Customer

Another common pitfall for startups is losing focus on the customer as they scale and grow. As startups become more successful and start to attract more attention and funding, it can be tempting to shift focus away from the core value proposition and towards new shiny objects or opportunities. But this can lead to a loss of customer trust and loyalty, and ultimately undermine the long-term success of the business.

To stay focused on the customer, startups need to prioritize customer feedback and insights at every stage of the journey. This means regularly soliciting input and feedback from customers, using that feedback to inform product and service improvements, and consistently communicating and engaging with customers to build strong relationships and loyalty over time.

3. Neglecting Company Culture

As startups scale and grow, it can be easy to neglect or deprioritize company culture in the pursuit of rapid growth and expansion. But a strong company culture is essential for attracting and retaining top talent, building a cohesive and motivated team, and creating a positive and productive work environment that supports long-term success.

To build and maintain a strong company culture, startups need to be intentional and proactive about defining and communicating their values, mission, and vision. They need to lead by example and model the behaviors and attitudes they want to see in their team, and create opportunities for team building, recognition, and growth. They also need to be willing to make tough decisions and trade-offs to protect and preserve the culture, even if it means sacrificing short-term gains or opportunities.

4. Failing to Adapt and Pivot

Finally, one of the biggest challenges that startups face as they scale is the need to constantly adapt and pivot in response to changing market conditions, customer needs, and competitive pressures. Startups that are too rigid or inflexible in their approach can quickly become irrelevant or obsolete, while those that are able to pivot and adapt can often find new opportunities for growth and success.

To be adaptable and responsive, startups need to foster a culture of experimentation and learning, where failure is seen as an opportunity for growth and improvement rather than a setback. They need to be data-driven and customer-centric in their decision-making, constantly testing and iterating based on real-world feedback and insights. And they need to be willing to make bold moves and take calculated risks when the opportunity arises, even if it means pivoting away from their original plan or vision.

Proven Scaling Strategies and Tactics

While there is no one-size-fits-all approach to scaling and growth, there are some proven strategies and tactics that successful startups have used to overcome challenges and achieve exponential growth. Here are some of the most effective scaling strategies and tactics:

1. Nail the Fundamentals

Before a startup can scale effectively, it needs to have a solid foundation in place. This means nailing the fundamentals of the business, from the value proposition and target market to the product and business model to the team and culture.

Startups that have a clear and compelling value proposition, a deep understanding of their target market and customer needs, and a product that solves a real problem and delivers real value are much more likely to succeed than those that don't. They also need to have a scalable and profitable business model, with clear unit economics and a path to long-term sustainability.

Finally, startups need to have a strong and cohesive team in place, with the right mix of skills, experience, and attitudes to support growth and success. This means hiring for fit as well as function, and creating a culture that values collaboration, innovation, and continuous learning.

2. Focus on the Core

As startups scale and grow, it can be tempting to try to do too many things at once or to chase after every new opportunity that arises. But successful startups know that focus is key, and that it's better to do a few things really well than to spread themselves too thin.

Startups that are able to focus on their core value proposition and target market, and ruthlessly prioritize their efforts and resources around that core, are much more likely to succeed than those that try to be everything to everyone. This means saying no to distractions and opportunities that don't align with the core mission and vision, and doubling down on the things that are working and driving real value for customers.

3. Leverage Partnerships and Ecosystems

Another effective scaling strategy is to leverage partnerships and ecosystems to expand reach, access new markets and customers, and tap into complementary skills and resources. Startups that are able to build strong relationships with key partners, suppliers, and customers can often achieve much more than they could on their own.

Partnerships can take many forms, from strategic alliances and joint ventures to channel partnerships and co-marketing initiatives. The key is to find partners that share similar values and goals, and that can provide mutual value and support for growth.

Startups can also benefit from participating in broader ecosystems and communities, such as industry associations, startup accelerators, and entrepreneurial networks. These ecosystems can provide access to mentorship, funding, and other resources, as well as opportunities for collaboration, learning, and exposure to new ideas and perspectives.

4. Invest in Marketing and Sales

To scale and grow effectively, startups need to invest in marketing and sales to reach and acquire new customers, build brand awareness and loyalty, and drive revenue growth. This means developing a clear and compelling marketing strategy, with a focus on the channels and tactics that are most effective for reaching and converting the target market.

Startups need to be data-driven and experimental in their approach to marketing, constantly testing and optimizing their campaigns and messages based on real-world results and feedback. They also need to invest in a strong and scalable sales organization, with the right mix of people, processes, and technology to support growth and efficiency.

Finally, startups need to be proactive and strategic in their approach to customer acquisition and retention, with a focus on building long-term relationships and loyalty over time. This means providing exceptional customer service and support, regularly soliciting feedback and input, and constantly innovating and improving the product and customer experience based on that feedback.

5. Embrace Technology and Automation

Finally, successful startups know that technology and automation can be powerful tools for scaling and growth, enabling them to do more with less and to focus their efforts and resources on the things that matter most.

Startups that are able to leverage technology and automation to streamline operations, improve efficiency, and enhance the customer experience are much more likely to succeed than those that rely on manual and inefficient processes. This means investing in the right tools and platforms, from customer relationship management (CRM) and marketing automation to financial management and analytics.

It also means being proactive and strategic in the use of data and analytics to inform decision-making and drive continuous improvement. Startups that are able to collect, analyze, and act on data in real-time are much better equipped to identify opportunities and challenges, and to adapt and pivot as needed to stay ahead of the curve.

Scaling Case Studies and Success Stories

To bring these scaling strategies and tactics to life, let's take a look at some real-world case studies and success stories of startups that have achieved exponential growth and success:

1. Airbnb

Airbnb is a classic example of a startup that was able to scale and grow rapidly by focusing on its core value proposition and leveraging partnerships and ecosystems to expand its reach and impact.

Founded in 2008 as a simple platform for people to rent out their spare rooms or apartments to travelers, Airbnb quickly grew into a global phenomenon, with millions of listings in over 190 countries. The key to Airbnb's success was its ability to tap into the growing trend of the sharing economy, and to provide a unique and compelling value proposition that resonated with both hosts and guests.

Airbnb also invested heavily in marketing and branding to build awareness and trust in its platform, and in technology and automation to streamline operations and improve the user experience. It also leveraged partnerships with local governments, tourism boards, and other key stakeholders to navigate regulatory challenges and expand into new markets.

Today, Airbnb is valued at over $100 billion and is widely regarded as one of the most successful and influential startups of the past decade.

2. Slack

Slack is another example of a startup that was able to achieve rapid growth and success by focusing on its core value proposition and leveraging technology and automation to improve collaboration and productivity for teams.

Founded in 2013 as a simple messaging app for teams, Slack quickly gained traction among startups and tech companies who were looking for a more efficient and effective way to communicate and collaborate. The key to Slack's success was its ability to provide a seamless and intuitive user experience, with features like channels, direct messages, and integrations with other tools and platforms.

Slack also invested heavily in marketing and sales to build awareness and adoption among its target market, and in partnerships and ecosystems to expand its reach and value proposition. It also embraced a freemium business model, offering a basic version of its product for free while charging for more advanced features and functionality.

Today, Slack is used by millions of users across the globe and is valued at over $20 billion, making it one of the most successful and influential startups of the past decade.

3. Zoom

Zoom is a more recent example of a startup that was able to achieve exponential growth and success by focusing on its core value proposition and leveraging technology and automation to provide a superior user experience for remote collaboration and communication.

Founded in 2011 as a simple video conferencing platform, Zoom quickly gained traction among businesses and individuals who were looking for a more reliable and user-friendly alternative to existing solutions like Skype and WebEx. The key to Zoom's success was its ability to provide a high-quality and seamless user experience, with features like HD video, screen sharing, and virtual backgrounds.

Zoom also invested heavily in marketing and partnerships to build awareness and adoption among its target market, and in technology and infrastructure to support its rapid growth and scale. It also embraced a freemium business model, offering a basic version of its product for free while charging for more advanced features and functionality.

Today, Zoom is used by millions of users across the globe and has become an essential tool for remote work and collaboration in the wake of the COVID-19 pandemic. It is valued at over $100 billion and is widely regarded as one of the most successful and influential startups of the past decade.

The Road to Unicorn Status

While not every startup will achieve the level of success and scale of companies like Airbnb, Slack, and Zoom, these examples provide valuable lessons and insights for entrepreneurs and investors who are looking to build and scale successful businesses.

One of the most important lessons is the importance of focus and prioritization. Successful startups are able to identify their core value proposition and target market, and ruthlessly prioritize their efforts and resources around that core. They resist the temptation to try to be everything to everyone, and instead double down on the things that are working and driving real value for customers.

Another key lesson is the importance of partnerships and ecosystems. Successful startups are able to build strong relationships with key partners, suppliers, and customers, and to leverage those relationships to expand their reach and impact. They also participate actively in broader ecosystems and communities, tapping into the collective knowledge and resources of their peers and mentors.

Finally, successful startups embrace technology and automation as key enablers of growth and scale. They invest in the right tools and platforms to streamline operations, improve efficiency, and enhance the user experience. They also use data and analytics to inform decision-making and drive continuous improvement, constantly testing and iterating based on real-world feedback and results.

By focusing on these key strategies and tactics, startups can increase their chances of achieving the kind of exponential growth and success that can lead to unicorn status and beyond. Of course, there are no guarantees in the world of startups, and even the most promising companies can face setbacks and challenges along the way.

But by staying true to their core values and mission, by constantly learning and adapting based on data and feedback, and by leveraging the power of partnerships and technology, startups can position themselves for long-term success and impact. And in doing so, they can not only achieve their own goals and aspirations, but also make a positive difference in the world and leave a lasting legacy for future generations.

Lessons from Nas: Building a Legacy of Success and Impact

As we've seen throughout this book, the journey of the Illmatic Investor is not just about achieving financial success and scale, but also about building a legacy of impact and influence that extends far beyond the bottom line.

And there is perhaps no better example of this than Nas himself, who has not only achieved incredible success and longevity in the music industry, but has also used his platform and resources to make a positive difference in the world and inspire countless others to do the same.

Throughout his career, Nas has embodied many of the same qualities and strategies that we've explored in this chapter on scaling and growth. He has stayed true to his core values and artistic vision, while constantly evolving and adapting his style and approach

Success Stories from Nas's Portfolio

As an investor, Nas has applied many of the same principles and strategies that have made him successful as a musician to his approach to startup investing. Through QVP, Nas has built an impressive portfolio of successful startups across a range of industries and sectors. Here are a few examples of some of his most notable investments:

1. Coinbase

One of Nas's most successful investments to date has been in Coinbase, the leading cryptocurrency exchange platform. Nas was an early investor in the company, participating in its Series B funding round in 2013 when it was still a relatively unknown startup.

Since then, Coinbase has grown into a global powerhouse, with millions of users and billions of dollars in trading volume. In April 2021, Coinbase went public through a direct listing on the Nasdaq, with a valuation of over $85 billion. Nas's early investment in the company has likely generated a significant return, showcasing his ability to identify and back promising startups in emerging industries.

2. Dropbox

Another notable investment in Nas's portfolio is Dropbox, the cloud storage and file sharing platform. Nas was an early investor in the company, participating in its Series B funding round in 2011.

Since then, Dropbox has grown into a major player in the cloud storage space, with over 700 million registered users and $1.6 billion in annual revenue. The company went public in 2018, with a valuation of over $8 billion. Nas's early investment in Dropbox has likely generated a strong return and further demonstrates his ability to identify promising startups in the tech industry.

3. Casper

Nas has also invested in Casper, the direct-to-consumer mattress and sleep products company. He participated in the company's Series B funding round in 2015, alongside other high-profile investors like 50 Cent and Adam Levine.

Since then, Casper has grown into a major player in the mattress industry, with over $400 million in annual revenue and a valuation of over $1 billion. The company went public in 2020, although its stock price has struggled in recent months. Despite this, Nas's investment in Casper demonstrates his willingness to back innovative startups in traditional industries like mattresses and sleep products.

These are just a few examples of the many successful investments in Nas's portfolio. Other notable companies he has backed include Lyft, Genius, Robinhood, and PillPack, among others. Through these investments, Nas has demonstrated his ability to identify and support promising startups across a range of industries and sectors, from tech and finance to healthcare and consumer products.

Pulling It All Together

Nas famously told us in his classic song, "It ain't hard to tell, I excel, then prevail, the mic is contacted, I attract clientele."

And in this soliloquy, he is showcasing his confidence and ability to succeed in the rap game.

"It ain't hard to tell, I excel, then prevail"

Here, Nas is asserting that his talent and success are evident to anyone who pays attention. He excels in his craft, and through his excellence, he prevails over his competition. This line is a testament to his unwavering self-belief and his determination to rise to the top of his field.

"The mic is contacted, I attract clientele."

In this line, Nas is referring to his ability to connect with his audience and build a loyal fan base. By "contacting" the microphone, he is delivering his message and showcasing his skills, which in turn attracts "clientele" – in this case, fans and listeners who appreciate and support his music.

As it relates to moving from startup to success, Nas's lyrics encapsulate the mindset and approach needed to take a startup venture from its early stages to a thriving, successful business. Just like Nas, entrepreneurs must have a strong belief in their own abilities and the determination to excel in their chosen field. They must be willing to put in the hard work and dedication required to prevail over the competition and establish themselves as leaders in their industry.

Additionally, Nas's emphasis on attracting clientele is directly applicable to the startup world. For a startup to succeed, it must be able to connect with its target audience and build a loyal customer base. This requires a deep understanding of customer needs, effective marketing and communication strategies, and the ability to deliver a product or service that resonates with the market.

Nas's collaboration with Hit-Boy is a prime example of this principle in action. By partnering with a talented young producer and creating music that speaks to their audience, Nas and Hit-Boy have been able to attract a dedicated fan base and achieve significant success in today's music industry. Their partnership mirrors the startup journey, where a great idea, combined with the right team and execution, can lead to remarkable growth and achievement.

In essence, Nas's lyric serves as a powerful reminder that success in any field, whether it's music or entrepreneurship, comes down to having confidence in your abilities, putting in the work to excel, and building strong connections with your audience or customers. By embodying these principles and staying focused on their goals, startups can navigate the challenges of growth and ultimately prevail in their chosen market, just as Nas has done throughout his illustrious career in the rap game.

Also, as we've seen throughout this chapter, scaling and growth are essential components of startup success. The journey from idea to unicorn status is never a straight line, but rather a winding path filled with challenges, setbacks, and opportunities. Successful startups are able to navigate this path by staying focused on their core value proposition, leveraging partnerships and ecosystems, investing in marketing and technology, and constantly learning and adapting based on data and feedback.

Nas's own journey as an investor provides a compelling case study of these principles in action. Through QVP, Nas has built an impressive portfolio of successful startups by applying the same skills and strategies that have made him a legendary musician: a keen eye for talent and potential, a willingness to take calculated risks, and a commitment to long-term vision and impact.

By backing companies like Coinbase, Dropbox, and Casper, Nas has demonstrated his ability to identify and support promising startups in a range of industries and sectors. He has also shown a willingness to leverage his own platform and resources to help these companies grow and succeed, whether through strategic advice, introductions to key partners and investors, or public endorsements and promotion.

But perhaps most importantly, Nas's approach to investing is grounded in a deep sense of purpose and responsibility. Like his music, his investments are not just about achieving financial success, but about making a positive impact on the world and leaving a lasting legacy for future generations.

As he has said in interviews, Nas sees investing as a way to create opportunities and empowerment for underrepresented communities, and to use his platform and resources to drive positive change. By backing startups that are solving real problems and creating value for customers and society, Nas is not only generating returns for himself and his investors, but also making a meaningful difference in the world.

For aspiring entrepreneurs and investors, Nas's journey offers a powerful example of what is possible when you combine skill, vision, and purpose. By staying true to your core values and mission, by constantly learning and evolving, and by leveraging the power of partnerships and technology, you too can achieve the kind of exponential growth and success that can change the world.

Of course, the road to startup success is never easy, and there will always be challenges and setbacks along the way. But as Nas has shown us time and again, the key is to stay focused on the bigger picture, to surround yourself with people who share your vision and values, and to never lose sight of the impact you want to make in the world.

So as we conclude this chapter on scaling and growth, let us take inspiration from the Illmatic Investor himself. Let us dream big, take bold risks, and use our skills and resources to create a better future for ourselves and for generations to come. Because in the end, that is the true measure of success – not just the size of our bank accounts or the valuations of our companies, but the positive impact we leave on the world and the legacy we build for those who come after us.

PART III: STRATEGIC INVESTMENTS - DIVERSIFYING BEYOND THE BASICS

CHAPTER 7

REPRESENT - REAL ESTATE AND OTHER ALTERNATIVE INVESTMENTS

"F#@k a yard, God, let me see a hundred grand, could use a gun, son, but f#@k being the wanted man."

The metaverse is a virtual shared space, created by the convergence of virtual reality, augmented reality, and the internet. It's a collective, immersive, and interactive online environment where users can engage with each other and digital objects in a way that mimics real-life interactions. In the metaverse, users can participate in various activities such as gaming, socializing, learning, and even trading virtual assets.

Non-fungible tokens (NFTs) are unique digital assets that are verified on a blockchain. They can represent ownership of digital items such as art, music, videos, or even virtual real estate within the metaverse. Each NFT is one-of-a-kind and cannot be exchanged for another identical item, hence the term "non-fungible."

Nas, known for his astute investment strategies, has demonstrated his foresight by investing in metaverse real estate through Everyrealm. By participating in the $60 million Series A financing round, Nas, along with other hip-hop artists like Lil Baby and Gunna, has shown confidence in the potential growth and value of virtual real estate. Everyrealm's holdings in 25 metaverse platforms and over 100 developed projects indicate a strong foothold in this emerging market. As the metaverse continues to evolve and attract more users, the value of virtual real estate is expected to increase, potentially providing significant returns for early investors like Nas.

In addition to his investment in Everyrealm, Nas has also partnered with Royal, a blockchain-powered platform that allows fans to invest in their favorite artists' music. By releasing extended versions of NFTs called limited digital assets, Nas is not only providing his fans with a unique opportunity to own a piece of his music but also exploring new avenues for monetizing his artistic creations. This move demonstrates Nas's understanding of the potential of blockchain technology and his willingness to embrace innovative ways of engaging with his audience.

Nas's investments in the metaverse and NFTs align with his broader strategy of diversifying his portfolio and exploring alternative investments. Just as he has invested in real-world real estate and startups, Nas recognizes the potential of the virtual world to generate significant returns. By getting in on the ground floor of these emerging technologies, Nas is positioning himself to benefit from their future growth and success.

As we've seen throughout this book, the world of investing is vast and multifaceted, offering a wide range of opportunities for those willing to think creatively and take calculated risks. While stocks and startups may be the most well-known and popular investment vehicles, they are far from the only options available to savvy investors looking to diversify their portfolios and maximize their returns.

In this chapter, we'll explore the realm of alternative investments, with a particular focus on real estate and other tangible assets that can provide a hedge against market volatility and inflation. We'll examine the unique characteristics and benefits of these investments, the strategies and best practices for navigating these markets, and the ways in which investors can incorporate these assets into their overall financial plans.

The Case for Alternative Investments

Before we dive into the specifics of real estate and other alternative investments, let's take a step back and consider the broader case for diversifying beyond traditional stocks and bonds.

Historically, the stock market has been one of the most reliable and effective ways to build long-term wealth. Over the past century, the S&P 500 has delivered an average annual return of around 10%, outpacing inflation and providing a solid foundation for retirement savings and other financial goals.

However, the stock market is also notoriously volatile and unpredictable, subject to sudden swings and corrections that can wipe out gains and leave investors feeling anxious and uncertain. In recent years, we've seen this volatility play out in real-time, with the COVID-19 pandemic and other global events sending shockwaves through financial markets and highlighting the risks of relying too heavily on any one asset class.

This is where alternative investments come in. By diversifying into assets like real estate, commodities, collectibles, and private equity, investors can potentially reduce their overall portfolio risk while still achieving attractive returns. These assets tend to have low correlations with traditional stocks and bonds, meaning they can provide a buffer against market downturns and help smooth out returns over time.

Alternative investments can also offer unique benefits and opportunities that may not be available through traditional securities. For example, real estate can provide a steady stream of rental income and the potential for long-term appreciation, while collectibles like art and wine can offer both aesthetic and financial value. Private equity and venture capital can provide exposure to high-growth companies and industries that may not be accessible through public markets.

Of course, alternative investments also come with their own set of risks and challenges. They can be less liquid than stocks and bonds, meaning they may be harder to buy and sell quickly. They can also be more complex and opaque, requiring specialized knowledge and due diligence to evaluate and manage effectively. And they may be subject to different regulatory and tax treatment than traditional securities, which can impact their overall returns and suitability for different investors.

Despite these challenges, many sophisticated investors have long recognized the value of alternative investments as part of a well-rounded portfolio. In fact, some of the most successful investors in history, from Warren Buffett to Yale's endowment fund, have made significant allocations to alternative assets as a way to manage risk and generate outsized returns.

As Nas himself has demonstrated through his own investment strategy, which includes a diverse mix of startups, real estate, and other alternative assets, the key is to approach these investments with a clear understanding of their unique characteristics and a disciplined, long-term mindset. By doing so, investors can potentially unlock new sources of value and build a more resilient, diversified portfolio that can weather any market conditions.

The Power of Real Estate Investing

One of the most popular and accessible alternative investments is real estate. From residential properties and apartment buildings to commercial offices and industrial warehouses, real estate offers a tangible, physical asset that can provide both income and appreciation over time.

The benefits of real estate investing are numerous. For one, real estate tends to be a relatively stable and predictable asset class, with a long history of steady returns and a low correlation to the stock market. This can make it an attractive option for investors looking to reduce their overall portfolio volatility and generate consistent cash flow.

Real estate also offers the potential for significant tax benefits, including deductions for mortgage interest, property taxes, and depreciation. These deductions can help offset the costs of owning and managing a property, and can even result in a negative effective tax rate for some investors.

Perhaps most importantly, real estate provides a tangible, physical asset that can appreciate in value over time. Unlike stocks or bonds, which are essentially just pieces of paper or digital entries, real estate is a real, concrete asset that can be touched, seen, and experienced. This can provide a sense of security and stability that is particularly appealing in times of economic uncertainty.

Of course, real estate investing is not without its challenges. Properties require ongoing maintenance and management, which can be time-consuming and expensive. Vacancies, tenant turnover, and unexpected repairs can eat into cash flow and returns. And real estate markets can be highly local and subject to their own unique risks and opportunities, requiring careful research and due diligence to navigate effectively.

Despite these challenges, many investors have found real estate to be a powerful tool for building long-term wealth and achieving their financial goals. And with the rise of new technologies and platforms like crowdfunding and real estate investment trusts (REITs), it has never been easier or more accessible for individual investors to get started in this asset class.

One popular strategy for investing in real estate is the "BRRRR" method, which stands for "Buy, Rehab, Rent, Refinance, Repeat." This approach involves purchasing a distressed or undervalued property, renovating it to increase its value and rental potential, renting it out to generate cash flow, and then refinancing the property to pull out equity and repeat the process with another property.

Another strategy is to focus on "house hacking," which involves purchasing a multi-unit property, living in one unit, and renting out the others to offset the mortgage and generate additional income. This can be a particularly attractive option for younger investors or those just starting out, as it allows them to build equity and cash flow while also providing a place to live.

For investors who prefer a more passive approach, REITs can offer exposure to a diversified portfolio of real estate assets without the hassle of direct ownership. REITs are publicly-traded companies that own and operate income-producing real estate, and they are required to distribute at least 90% of their taxable income to shareholders in the form of dividends. This can provide a steady stream of income and the potential for capital appreciation, while also offering greater liquidity and transparency than direct real estate ownership.

Ultimately, the key to success in real estate investing is to approach it with a clear strategy and a long-term mindset. By carefully evaluating properties, managing risks, and staying disciplined in the face of market fluctuations, investors can potentially build significant wealth and achieve their financial goals through this powerful alternative asset class.

Exploring Other Alternative Investments

While real estate may be one of the most well-known and accessible alternative investments, it is far from the only option available to investors looking to diversify their portfolios. In fact, there is a wide range of alternative assets that can offer unique benefits and opportunities, from commodities and collectibles to private equity and hedge funds.

One popular alternative investment is commodities, which are physical goods like gold, oil, and agricultural products that are traded on global markets. Commodities can provide a hedge against inflation and currency fluctuations, as well as exposure to global economic trends and supply and demand dynamics. They can also offer diversification benefits, as they tend to have low correlations with stocks and bonds.

Another alternative investment that has gained popularity in recent years is collectibles, such as art, wine, and rare coins. These assets can offer both aesthetic and financial value, and can be particularly attractive to investors with a passion for a particular hobby or interest. Collectibles can also provide a hedge against inflation, as their value tends to appreciate over time and is not directly tied to the performance of financial markets.

Private equity and venture capital are another set of alternative investments that can offer exposure to high-growth companies and industries. These investments involve providing capital to private companies in exchange for an ownership stake, with the goal of generating significant returns through an eventual exit or liquidity event. Private equity and venture capital can be particularly attractive to investors with a high risk tolerance and a long-term investment horizon, as they often require significant capital commitments and can take several years to generate returns.

Hedge funds are another type of alternative investment that have gained popularity among sophisticated investors. These funds use a wide range of strategies to generate returns, from long/short equity and global macro to distressed debt and arbitrage. Hedge funds can offer the potential for high returns and low correlations with traditional asset classes, but they also come with high fees and minimum investment requirements that can make them inaccessible to many individual investors.

Other alternative investments that may be worth considering include farmland and timber, which can provide exposure to the agricultural and forestry sectors, as well as infrastructure and energy assets, which can offer steady cash flows and the potential for long-term appreciation.

Ultimately, the key to successfully investing in alternative assets is to approach them with the same level of discipline and due diligence as traditional securities. This means carefully evaluating the risks and potential rewards of each investment, understanding the unique characteristics and drivers of each asset class, and staying disciplined in the face of market fluctuations and uncertainty.

It also means being realistic about the liquidity and accessibility of these investments, and ensuring that they are appropriate for your overall financial situation and goals. Alternative investments can be a powerful tool for diversifying your portfolio and generating attractive returns, but they should not be viewed as a replacement for a well-rounded investment strategy that includes traditional stocks and bonds.

Building a Diversified Portfolio with Alternative Investments

So how can investors effectively incorporate alternative investments into their overall portfolio strategy? The key is to take a holistic, diversified approach that balances risk and reward across a range of asset classes and investment vehicles.

One common approach is to use alternative investments as a way to complement and enhance a core portfolio of stocks and bonds. For example, an investor might allocate a portion of their portfolio to real estate or commodities as a way to hedge against inflation and generate additional income, while still maintaining a significant allocation to traditional securities for long-term growth and stability.

Another approach is to use alternative investments as a way to tap into specific market opportunities or trends that may not be accessible through public markets. For example, an investor might allocate a portion of their portfolio to private equity or venture capital as a way to gain exposure to high-growth startups or emerging industries, while still maintaining a diversified mix of traditional assets.

Regardless of the specific approach, the key is to ensure that alternative investments are integrated into a broader investment strategy that is aligned with your financial goals, risk tolerance, and time horizon. This means carefully considering the role that each investment plays in your overall portfolio, and ensuring that you have the knowledge and resources necessary to effectively manage and monitor these assets over time.

It also means being mindful of the fees and expenses associated with alternative investments, which can be higher than traditional securities and can eat into overall returns. Investors should carefully evaluate the costs and benefits of each investment, and ensure that they are getting value for the fees they are paying.

Finally, it's important to remember that alternative investments are not a magic bullet or a guarantee of success. Like any investment, they come with their own set of risks and challenges, and there is no substitute for careful research, disciplined investing, and a long-term perspective.

That being said, for investors who are willing to put in the work and take a thoughtful, diversified approach, alternative investments can be a powerful tool for building wealth and achieving financial goals over time. By tapping into the unique opportunities and characteristics of these assets, investors can potentially enhance their returns, reduce their overall portfolio risk, and build a more resilient, flexible investment strategy that can weather any market conditions.

Real-World Examples and Case Studies

To bring the concept of alternative investing to life, let's take a look at a few real-world examples and case studies of investors who have successfully incorporated these assets into their portfolios.

One notable example is the Yale University endowment fund, which has long been a pioneer in alternative investing. Under the leadership of

David Swensen, who served as the fund's chief investment officer from 1985 until his passing in 2021, the Yale endowment consistently generated strong returns and outperformed its peers by investing heavily in alternative assets like private equity, venture capital, and real estate.

Swensen's approach was based on the idea that alternative investments could provide greater diversification, higher potential returns, and a better alignment of interests between investors and managers than traditional public securities. By carefully selecting top-tier managers and maintaining a long-term, disciplined approach, Swensen and his team were able to build a portfolio that generated an average annual return of 12.4% over the past three decades, far outpacing the performance of most other endowments and pension funds.

Another example of successful alternative investing is the Blackstone Group, one of the world's largest private equity firms. Founded in 1985 by Stephen Schwarzman and Peter Peterson, Blackstone has built a reputation for delivering strong returns to its investors by focusing on a wide range of alternative assets, from real estate and infrastructure to hedge funds and credit.

One of Blackstone's most notable investments was its 2007 acquisition of Hilton Hotels for $26 billion, which it subsequently took public in 2013 for a valuation of over $12 billion. Through a combination of operational improvements, strategic acquisitions, and effective capital management, Blackstone was able to generate significant value for its investors and cement its position as a leader in the alternative investment space.

Finally, let's take a look at Nas himself, who has built a successful career as both a musician and an investor by taking a creative, diverse approach to his financial strategy. In addition to his ventures in the music industry,

Nas has made significant investments in a wide range of alternative assets, from real estate and art to startups and cryptocurrencies.

Besides his notable investment in The Metaverse and NFT's as mentioned at the beginning of this chapter, Nas has also been an active investor in real estate, with a particular focus on properties in his native New York City. In 2021, he partnered with brokerage firm Avenue Realty Capital to launch a $20 million fund to invest in affordable housing and community development projects in underserved neighborhoods.

These examples demonstrate the power and potential of alternative investing, and the ways in which investors can use these assets to build wealth, create value, and make a positive impact in the world. By taking a thoughtful, disciplined approach and staying true to their own unique vision and values, investors like Swensen, Schwarzman, and Nas have been able to navigate the complex world of alternative investing and achieve significant success over time.

Conclusion and Key Takeaways

As we've seen throughout this chapter, alternative investments can be a powerful tool for investors looking to diversify their portfolios, generate attractive returns, and tap into unique opportunities beyond the traditional world of stocks and bonds.

From real estate and commodities to private equity and hedge funds, these assets offer a wide range of benefits and characteristics that can help investors build wealth, manage risk, and achieve their long-term financial goals. They can provide a hedge against inflation and market volatility, generate steady cash flows and capital appreciation, and offer exposure to high-growth companies and industries that may not be accessible through public markets.

At the same time, alternative investments also come with their own set of risks and challenges, from illiquidity and complexity to high fees and minimum investment requirements. They require careful research, due diligence, and ongoing management to effectively navigate and optimize over time.

For investors looking to incorporate alternative investments into their portfolios, there are a few key takeaways to keep in mind:

1. Take a diversified, holistic approach: Alternative investments should be viewed as a complement to, not a replacement for, traditional stocks and bonds. By integrating these assets into a broader, diversified portfolio strategy, investors can potentially enhance their returns and manage risk more effectively over time.

2. Understand the risks and characteristics of each asset class: Each type of alternative investment comes with its own unique set of risks, drivers, and potential rewards. Before investing, it's important to carefully evaluate the specific characteristics of each asset class and ensure that they align with your overall financial goals and risk tolerance.

3. Work with experienced, trusted partners: Alternative investments can be complex and opaque, and often require specialized expertise to effectively manage and optimize. By working with experienced, trusted partners like investment advisors, fund managers, and industry experts, investors can gain access to the knowledge, resources, and networks needed to succeed in these markets.

4. Stay disciplined and focused on the long-term: Like any investment, alternative assets are subject to short-term fluctuations and uncertainties. To generate consistent, attractive returns over time, it's important to stay disciplined, maintain a long-term perspective, and avoid making impulsive decisions based on short-term market movements.

5. Align investments with values and impact: Finally, as Nas and other impact-focused investors have demonstrated, alternative investments can be a powerful tool for aligning financial goals with broader social and environmental values. By investing in assets like affordable housing, sustainable agriculture, and community development projects, investors can potentially generate both financial returns and positive impact in the world.

Ultimately, the world of alternative investing is vast, complex, and full of both opportunities and challenges. But for investors who are willing to put in the work, take a thoughtful, disciplined approach, and stay true to their own unique vision and values, these assets can be a powerful tool for building wealth, creating value, and making a difference in the world.

As the legendary investor Warren Buffett once said, "I don't look to jump over 7-foot bars; I look around for 1-foot bars that I can step over." In the world of investing, alternative assets may often seem like high hurdles or complex obstacles. But by taking a creative, opportunistic approach and staying focused on the long-term, investors can find their own unique path to success and make their mark on the world, one investment at a time.

Based on the information provided, here are some key points about Nas's diversification strategies as an investor:

Nas has invested in a wide range of alternative assets beyond just stocks and startups. Some examples include:

- Real estate: Nas has invested in properties in his native New York City, including partnering on a $20 million fund to invest in affordable housing and community development projects. Real estate can provide steady rental income and long-term appreciation.

- Media and content: Nas invested in the media company Mass Appeal in 2013. It has grown into a diversified platform spanning music, podcasts, documentaries, live events and more. This allows him to leverage his expertise in music and entertainment.

- Art and collectibles: Nas is known to collect art as an alternative investment that can appreciate in value over time.

- Cryptocurrencies: As an early adopter, Nas has invested in various cryptocurrency projects and platforms.

The key takeaways are that Nas takes a creative, opportunistic approach to diversifying his investments across asset classes. He looks for unique opportunities to generate returns while aligning with his interests and values. For example, affordable housing combines a societal impact with a financial return.

By thoughtfully allocating capital to both traditional and alternative investments, Nas demonstrates how diversification, when done strategically, can be a powerful wealth-building tool. While alternatives like real estate, private equity, and collectibles aren't accessible to everyone, the principles of exploring opportunities beyond public stocks and bonds still apply.

Ultimately, Nas provides a model for how to build a robust portfolio by staying open-minded, thinking long-term, and balancing financial goals with personal passions and social impact. His investment strategy, like his music, is about adapting and staying ahead of the curve. Aspiring investors can follow his lead by defining their own criteria and patiently cultivating a diverse asset mix to achieve their goals.

Pulling It All Together

When it was time to "Represent," Nas exclaimed, "F#@k a yard, God, let me see a hundred grand, could use a gun, son, but f#@k being the wanted man." This is him expressing his desire for financial success and the temptation to achieve it by any means necessary, including illegal activities. However, he ultimately rejects the idea of resorting to violence or crime, recognizing the consequences of being a "wanted man." Let's break it down and tie it to real estate and other alternative investments.

"F#@k a yard, God, let me see a hundred grand"

Here, Nas is saying that he doesn't care about having a traditional symbol of success, like a yard (which represents homeownership). Instead, he wants to see a large sum of money ($100,000). This line highlights his ambition and his focus on financial gain over material possessions.

"Could use a gun, son, but f#@k being the wanted man"

In this line, Nas acknowledges that he could resort to using a gun (i.e., violence or crime) to achieve his financial goals. However, he immediately rejects this idea, saying "f#@k being the wanted man." He recognizes that engaging in criminal activities would make him a target for law enforcement and ultimately hinder his ability to enjoy his success.

Tying it to real estate and alternative investments, Nas's lyric underscores the importance of pursuing financial success through legitimate means, rather than resorting to illegal activities. In the context of real estate and alternative investments, this means focusing on strategic, above-board investments that can generate long-term wealth and stability.

Real estate, in particular, has long been a popular investment vehicle for those seeking to build wealth and create a legacy. By investing in property, whether residential or commercial, individuals can benefit from potential appreciation, rental income, and tax advantages. Real estate also provides a tangible asset that can be passed down to future generations, creating a foundation for generational wealth.

Similarly, alternative investments such as venture capital, private equity, and even the emerging fields of the metaverse and NFTs offer the potential for significant returns, albeit with higher risk. By diversifying his portfolio and exploring these alternative investment opportunities, Nas is demonstrating his understanding of the importance of creating multiple streams of income and building wealth through legitimate means.

Aditionally, Nas's rejection of the "wanted man" lifestyle in favor of legal, above-board investments speaks to the importance of maintaining a clean record and a positive reputation in the business world. As an investor, particularly in the public eye, maintaining integrity and avoiding legal entanglements is crucial for long-term success and the ability to attract partners, investors, and opportunities.

In essence, Nas's lyric serves as a reminder that the pursuit of financial success should be grounded in legitimate, strategic investments rather than illicit activities. By focusing on real estate and other alternative investments, and maintaining a clean record and positive reputation, individuals can build lasting wealth and create a legacy that extends far beyond their own lifetimes. Nas's own journey from the streets to successful entrepreneur and investor exemplifies this principle, showing that with hard work, determination, and a commitment to doing things the right way, anyone can achieve their financial goals and create a better future for themselves and their community.

Also, In this chapter, we've seen how alternative investments beyond stocks and startups can play a vital role in a well-rounded portfolio. From real estate to private equity to collectibles, these assets offer unique ways to diversify holdings, generate income, and capture long-term appreciation.

The key is to approach alternatives with the same rigor and discipline as any other investment. That means understanding the specific risks and characteristics of each asset class, thinking holistically about how they fit into an overall financial plan, and relying on trusted partners for guidance and expertise.

While alternatives aren't appropriate for everyone, Nas's own diversification strategies illustrate how these investments can align with both financial and personal goals. His portfolio reflects his roots in music and media, his commitment to social impact, and his eye for emerging trends and technologies.

For investors seeking to follow Nas's lead, the lesson is to stay curious, open-minded and opportunistic. Define your own criteria for what makes an investment worthwhile - whether it's steady income, long-term growth, or the chance to own a piece of history. Then gradually diversify your holdings as you build knowledge and conviction.

As with any investment, a long-term mindset is essential. Alternative assets are often illiquid and take time to bear fruit. But for those willing to do the legwork and stay the course, the potential rewards can be substantial - both financially and personally.

Nas's journey from a kid in the Queensbridge projects to a successful entrepreneur and investor is a testament to the power of creativity, hustle and vision. By expanding his repertoire beyond music to include a broad range of alternative investments, he's built a portfolio that reflects his unique voice and values.

Ultimately, that's what distinguishes the true innovators and iconoclasts in any field - the ability to see opportunity where others see obstacles, and the conviction to forge their own path to success. With the right mindset and approach, we can all channel our inner Nas and build a financial future as rich and varied as the world around us.

CHAPTER 8

MEMORY LANE - LEARNING FROM FAILURES AND SUCCESSES

"Start off the dice-rollin' match, from craps to ceelo
With side-bets, so roll a deuce, nothin' below."

Throughout the history of hip-hop, there have been numerous instances of artists and celebrities making ill-advised investments, often falling victim to hype and the allure of quick profits. One notable example is MC Hammer, who, at the peak of his career in the early 1990s, had an estimated net worth of over $30 million. However, Hammer's lavish spending and poor investment choices, including a failed tech startup called DanceJam.com, led to his financial downfall. He eventually filed for bankruptcy in 1996, owing over $13 million to creditors.

Another cautionary tale is that of T-Pain, who, despite his successful music career, found himself in financial trouble due to a series of bad investments. In an interview, T-Pain revealed that he had lost a significant amount of money investing in real estate during the housing market crash of 2008. He also admitted to making impulsive purchases, such as buying a $1.2 million car, which depreciated in value quickly. These experiences highlight the importance of thorough research, due diligence, and a long-term investment strategy, rather than succumbing to hype and short-term gratification.

However, it's important to recognize that even the most savvy and successful investors can experience setbacks and failures. Jay-Z, widely regarded as one of the most successful hip-hop entrepreneurs, has also had his share of investment missteps. In 2007, he invested in a hotel development project in New York City that ultimately fell through, costing him millions of dollars. Similarly, 50 Cent, known for his successful business ventures like Vitamin Water, also experienced losses when he invested in a failed film project and a luxury headphone brand that didn't take off.

These examples demonstrate that failure is a natural part of the investment journey, and even the most successful individuals are not immune to it. The key, as Nas has demonstrated throughout his legendary career, is to learn from these experiences, adapt, and continue to make informed decisions based on sound research and a clear understanding of one's financial goals and risk tolerance. By approaching investments with a level-headed, long-term perspective and avoiding the pitfalls of hype and impulsive decision-making, aspiring investors can increase their chances of success and build lasting wealth, even in the face of occasional setbacks.

In this chapter, we'll take a trip down memory lane, exploring some of the most notable successes and setbacks in the world of investing. From the epic rise and fall of Theranos to the visionary bets of Warren Buffett and Charlie Munger, we'll examine the key lessons and takeaways that can help us become better, more resilient investors over time. We'll also look at some of the setbacks and challenges that Nas himself has faced in his investing career, and how he's used these experiences to refine his approach and build a stronger, more diversified portfolio.

The Rise and Fall of Theranos

One of the most dramatic and cautionary tales in recent investing history is the story of Theranos, the blood-testing startup that was once hailed as a revolutionary force in healthcare. Founded in 2003 by then-19-year-old Elizabeth Holmes, Theranos claimed to have developed groundbreaking technology that could run a full range of medical tests using just a few drops of blood from a finger prick.

The company's vision was compelling: by making blood testing faster, cheaper, and more accessible, Theranos promised to democratize healthcare and save countless lives around the world. Holmes, with her signature black turtleneck and deep baritone voice, became a media darling and a symbol of Silicon Valley's disruptive potential. She graced the covers of Forbes and Fortune, and was even named one of Time magazine's 100 most influential people in the world.

At its peak in 2014, Theranos was valued at over $9 billion, making Holmes the youngest self-made female billionaire in history. The company had raised over $700 million from a star-studded list of investors, including Oracle founder Larry Ellison, media mogul Rupert Murdoch, and former Secretary of State Henry Kissinger. It had also struck partnerships with major retailers like Walgreens and Safeway, with plans to roll out its testing services to thousands of locations nationwide.

But behind the hype and the accolades, there were signs that all was not well at Theranos. The company was notoriously secretive about its technology, refusing to publish peer-reviewed studies or allow outside experts to validate its claims. Employees who raised concerns about the accuracy and reliability of the company's tests were often silenced or fired. And despite Holmes's promises, Theranos struggled to deliver on its vision, with many of its tests proving to be unreliable or outright fraudulent.

The house of cards finally came crashing down in 2015, when a series of investigative reports by the Wall Street Journal revealed the extent of Theranos's deception. The company had been using traditional blood-testing machines for most of its tests, not its own proprietary technology. It had also been falsifying and manipulating data to make its tests appear more accurate than they really were. The revelations sparked a cascade of legal and regulatory challenges, with Holmes and her company facing charges of fraud from the SEC, the Department of Justice, and multiple state attorneys general.

In the end, Theranos was forced to shut down, with its investors losing hundreds of millions of dollars and its partners left to deal with the fallout. In January 2022, Holmes was convicted on four counts of wire fraud and conspiracy to commit wire fraud, related to defrauding investors. She was acquitted on charges of defrauding patients. In November 2022, Holmes was sentenced to 11 years and 3 months in prison. Additionally, Holmes and her former business partner, Ramesh "Sunny" Balwani, were ordered to pay $452 million in restitution to the victims of their fraudulent scheme.

The story of Theranos has become a cautionary tale for investors, entrepreneurs, and the public at large - a stark reminder of the dangers of hype, secrecy, and unchecked ambition in the world of startups and investing.

So what can we learn from the rise and fall of Theranos?

Here are a few key takeaways:

1. Be wary of hype and secrecy: If a company is making grandiose claims but refuses to provide evidence or allow outside validation, that's a major red flag. Transparency and accountability are essential for building trust and credibility with investors and the public.

2. Don't ignore warning signs: If employees, experts, or journalists are raising concerns about a company's practices or technology, take those concerns seriously. Don't let the fear of missing out on a hot investment opportunity cloud your judgment or override your due diligence.

3. Focus on fundamentals: At the end of the day, a company's success depends on its ability to deliver real value to customers and generate sustainable profits. Don't get caught up in the hype around a charismatic founder or a revolutionary vision - focus on the fundamentals of the business and the market it serves.

4. Diversify your portfolio: No matter how promising an investment opportunity may seem, it's always wise to spread your bets and not put all your eggs in one basket. By diversifying across different industries, asset classes, and risk profiles, you can help protect yourself against catastrophic losses if one of your investments goes south.

The Visionary Bets of Buffett and Munger

On the other end of the spectrum from Theranos are the visionary bets of Warren Buffett and Charlie Munger, the legendary investors behind Berkshire Hathaway. Over the course of their decades-long partnership, Buffett and Munger have built one of the most successful and admired investment firms in history, with a track record of consistent, market-beating returns and a reputation for integrity, discipline, and long-term thinking.

One of the keys to Buffett and Munger's success has been their willingness to make bold, contrarian bets on companies and industries that others have overlooked or dismissed. They've consistently identified undervalued assets and held onto them for the long haul, even in the face of market volatility or short-term setbacks. Some of their most notable investments include:

1. American Express: In 1964, Buffett invested $13 million in American Express, which was reeling from a massive fraud scandal involving its subsidiary, the Allied Crude Vegetable Oil Company. Despite the negative headlines and the company's tarnished reputation, Buffett saw value in American Express's core business and brand. He held onto his shares for decades, eventually reaping billions in profits as the company recovered and thrived.

2. Coca-Cola: In 1988, Buffett began acquiring shares in Coca-Cola, eventually building a stake that would come to be worth over $17 billion. He was attracted to the company's strong brand, global reach, and consistent profitability, even in the face of changing consumer tastes and economic headwinds. Today, Coca-Cola remains one of Berkshire Hathaway's largest and most iconic holdings.

3. Apple: In 2016, Berkshire Hathaway made a surprise investment in Apple, acquiring over $1 billion worth of shares in the tech giant. The move was notable because Buffett had long been skeptical of technology companies, preferring to invest in more traditional industries like insurance, retail, and manufacturing. But he saw value in Apple's loyal customer base, strong brand, and ability to generate consistent cash flows. As of 2021, Berkshire Hathaway's stake in Apple is worth over $120 billion, making it the firm's largest holding.

So what can we learn from Buffett and Munger's visionary approach to investing?

Here are a few key takeaways:

1. Think long-term: Buffett and Munger are famous for their patient, long-term approach to investing. They're not interested in chasing short-term gains or timing the market - instead, they focus on identifying high-quality companies with sustainable competitive advantages and holding onto them for years or even decades.

2. Be contrarian: Some of Buffett and Munger's most successful investments have come from going against the crowd and betting on companies that others have overlooked or dismissed. By doing their own research and trusting their instincts, they've been able to identify undervalued assets and reap outsized returns over time.

3. Focus on fundamentals: Like Nas, Buffett and Munger are disciplined investors who focus on the underlying fundamentals of a business - things like revenue growth, profitability, cash flow, and competitive moats. They're not swayed by hype or short-term fluctuations, but instead look for companies with strong, sustainable business models and talented management teams.

4. Stay within your circle of competence: One of Buffett's famous investing principles is to stay within his "circle of competence" - that is, to only invest in companies and industries that he understands well. By sticking to what he knows and not overextending himself, he's been able to avoid costly mistakes and build a portfolio of high-quality, reliable investments.

Learning from Nas's Setbacks and Successes

Of course, no discussion of investing failures and successes would be complete without examining the experiences of Nas himself. Throughout his career as both a musician and an investor, Nas has faced his share of setbacks and challenges, but he's also had some remarkable successes that have cemented his status as a visionary and a leader in the world of business and finance.

One of Nas's most high-profile setbacks came in the early 2000s, when he was embroiled in a bitter feud with fellow rapper Jay-Z. The feud started with a series of diss tracks and public insults, but it quickly escalated into a full-blown battle for supremacy in the hip-hop world. Nas's 2001 album "Stillmatic" was seen as a direct response to Jay-Z's attacks, and it included the scathing diss track "Ether," which many fans and critics saw as a decisive victory for Nas.

But the feud took a toll on Nas's career and his personal life. He later admitted that the constant negativity and drama had left him feeling drained and disillusioned with the music industry. He also faced financial setbacks during this period, with his record label Columbia reportedly pressuring him to release more commercial, radio-friendly music in order to recoup their investment.

Despite these challenges, Nas persevered and eventually emerged stronger and more focused than ever. He continued to release critically acclaimed albums throughout the 2000s and 2010s, cementing his status as one of the greatest rappers of all time. He also began to diversify his business interests, investing in a range of startups and ventures beyond the music industry.

One of Nas's most notable successes as an investor came in 2013, when he made an early-stage investment in a little-known startup called Coinbase. At the time, Coinbase was a fledgling cryptocurrency exchange with just a handful of employees and a few thousand users. But Nas saw the potential in the company and the broader cryptocurrency market, and he decided to take a chance on the young startup.

Fast forward, Coinbase is now one of the most valuable and influential companies in the crypto space, with a market capitalization of over $85 billion and millions of users worldwide. Nas's early investment in the company has paid off handsomely, with his stake now worth hundreds of millions of dollars.

But Nas's success with Coinbase is just one example of his broader approach to investing, which is grounded in a deep understanding of technology, culture, and social impact. Through QVP, Nas has backed a wide range of startups and initiatives, from music streaming services like Genius and Mass Appeal to ed-tech platforms like Quizlet and Wonderschool.

What sets Nas apart as an investor is his ability to identify and support companies that are not just financially promising, but also culturally relevant and socially impactful. He's not interested in chasing the latest fads or making a quick buck - instead, he looks for opportunities to create lasting value and drive positive change in the world.

So what can we learn from Nas's investing journey, with all its ups and downs?

Here are a few key takeaways:

1. **Embrace failure as a learning opportunity:** Like any successful investor, Nas has had his share of setbacks and losses over the years. But he doesn't let these failures define him - instead, he uses them as opportunities to learn, grow, and improve his approach.

2. **Stay true to your values and vision:** Throughout his career, Nas has remained committed to his core values and artistic vision, even in the face of pressure from record labels, critics, and the broader music industry. As an investor, he brings that same integrity and authenticity to his work, backing companies and causes that align with his personal mission and beliefs.

3. **Think beyond the obvious:** Some of Nas's most successful investments, like Coinbase, have come from identifying opportunities in emerging industries and technologies that others have overlooked or dismissed. By staying curious, open-minded, and willing to take calculated risks, he's been able to stay ahead of the curve and reap outsized rewards.

4. **Focus on impact as well as returns:** For Nas, investing isn't just about making money - it's about using his platform and resources to create positive change in the world. Whether he's backing initiatives to support underserved communities or investing in companies that are driving social and environmental progress, Nas sees his work as an investor as a way to leave a lasting legacy and make a real difference in people's lives.

5. Surround yourself with a strong team and network: Finally, Nas understands the importance of building a strong team and network of advisors, mentors, and collaborators. Through QVP and his various business ventures, he's built a highly effective ecosystem of partners and specialists who share his vision and values. By surrounding himself with smart, talented people who complement his own skills and expertise, he's been able to achieve more than he ever could alone.

Pulling It All Together

Nas told us earlier that Life is a B**ch but regardless of that you must take your chances! When he rapped, "Start off the dice-rollin' match, from craps to ceelo, with side-bets, so roll a deuce, nothin' below," he was using gambling terminology to illustrate the high-stakes nature of life and the importance of learning from both successes and failures. Let's break it down and tie it to the concept of learning from experiences in the investing world.

"Start off the dice-rollin' match, from craps to ceelo"

Here, Nas is referencing two popular dice games: craps and ceelo. By starting off the "dice-rollin' match," he's signaling the beginning of a high-stakes competition or challenge. This can be seen as a metaphor for the start of any new venture or investment opportunity.

"With side-bets, so roll a deuce, nothin' below"

In this line, Nas is emphasizing the importance of setting a minimum standard for success. In dice games, a "deuce" is a two, and by saying "nothin' below," he's indicating that he won't accept anything less than this minimum outcome. The mention of side-bets further underscores the high-stakes nature of the game.

Just like in gambling, investing involves taking calculated risks in the hopes of achieving a desired outcome but let me be clear Investing in NOT gambling! And just like in dice games, there are bound to be both wins and losses along the way. The key is to learn from these experiences and use them to inform future decisions.

When an investment succeeds, it's important to analyze the factors that contributed to that success. This could include things like thorough research, a solid understanding of market trends, or a well-timed entry point. By identifying these positive elements, investors can seek to replicate them in future endeavors, increasing their chances of continued success.

On the flip side, when an investment fails, it's equally important to examine what went wrong. This could be due to factors such as inadequate due diligence, overhyped expectations, or external market forces beyond one's control. By honestly assessing these missteps, investors can learn valuable lessons and adjust their strategies to mitigate similar risks in the future.

Nas's mention of "nothin' below" a deuce also speaks to the importance of setting realistic expectations and defining a minimum acceptable outcome. In investing, this could translate to establishing clear profit targets, defining risk tolerance levels, or setting stop-loss orders to limit potential downside. By having these guidelines in place, investors can make more informed decisions and avoid getting caught up in the heat of the moment.

The idea of "side-bets" in Nas's lyric can be seen as a nod to the concept of diversification in investing. By spreading one's bets across multiple opportunities, investors can potentially mitigate the impact of any single failure and increase their overall chances of success. This is similar to how gamblers might hedge their bets by placing wagers on multiple outcomes.

In essence, Nas's lyric serves as a reminder that success in any high-stakes endeavor, whether it's gambling or investing, requires a willingness to take calculated risks, learn from both successes and failures, and adapt one's approach based on those experiences. By setting clear expectations, defining acceptable outcomes, and diversifying one's bets, investors can navigate the ups and downs of the market and ultimately emerge stronger and wiser on the other side.

As we've seen throughout this chapter, the road to investing success is rarely a straight line. Even the most talented and experienced investors face setbacks, challenges, and failures along the way. The key is to learn from these experiences and use them as opportunities to grow, adapt, and improve over time.

Through the cautionary tale of Theranos, we've seen the dangers of hype, secrecy, and unchecked ambition in the world of startups and investing. We've learned the importance of focusing on fundamentals, diversifying our portfolios, and maintaining a healthy skepticism towards grandiose claims and promises.

From the visionary bets of Warren Buffett and Charlie Munger, we've gained insights into the power of long-term thinking, contrarian investing, and staying within our circle of competence. We've seen how a disciplined, patient approach to investing can lead to outsized returns and enduring success over time.

And through the experiences of Nas himself, we've witnessed the importance of resilience, authenticity, and a commitment to social impact in the face of adversity and setbacks. We've learned to embrace failure as a learning opportunity, to think beyond the obvious, and to build strong teams and networks that can help us achieve our goals.

Ultimately, the key lesson of this chapter is that investing is not just a technical skill or a financial discipline - it's a deeply human endeavor that requires emotional intelligence, moral integrity, and a willingness to confront our own limitations and biases. By studying the successes and failures of others, and by reflecting on our own experiences and values, we can become better, more resilient investors over time.

Of course, this is not to say that investing is easy or that success is guaranteed. As the legendary investor Benjamin Graham once said, "the investor's chief problem - and even his worst enemy - is likely to be himself." We are all vulnerable to the siren songs of greed, fear, and herd mentality, and it takes constant vigilance and self-awareness to stay true to our principles and strategies in the face of market volatility and uncertainty.

But by learning from the examples of visionary investors like Nas, Buffett, and Munger, and by staying focused on our own unique goals and values, we can build portfolios and legacies that stand the test of time. We can use our financial capital to drive positive change in the world, and we can inspire others to follow in our footsteps and pursue their own paths to success and fulfillment.

So as we move forward on our own investing journeys, let us take a moment to reflect on the lessons of this chapter and the examples of those who have come before us. Let us embrace the challenges and setbacks that inevitably come our way, and use them as fuel for our own growth and transformation. And let us never lose sight of the deeper purpose and meaning behind our work as investors - to create value, to drive progress, and to leave the world a little bit better than we found it.

In the end, that is the true measure of success in investing and in life - not just the size of our bank accounts or the trophies on our shelves, but the impact we have on the lives of others and the legacy we leave behind. So let us strive to be the best versions of ourselves, both as investors and as human beings. Let us learn from the past, seize the opportunities of the present, and build a future that is worthy of our highest aspirations and deepest values. That is the true art of the Illmatic Investor, and it is a journey that we are all called to take.

CONCLUSION

IF I RULED THE WORLD - ENVISIONING YOUR FINANCIAL FUTURE

"Imagine everybody flashin' fashion, designer clothes Lacing your clique up with diamond Rol's."

As we come to the end of this journey through the world of investing, it's important to take a step back and reflect on the bigger picture. What are we ultimately trying to achieve through our investments, and how can we ensure that our financial strategies are aligned with our deepest values and aspirations?

For Nas, the answer to this question has always been clear. From his early days as a young rapper in the Queensbridge projects to his later years as a successful entrepreneur and investor, Nas has always been driven by a sense of purpose and a desire to create a better world for himself, his family, and his community. His music has been a powerful tool for social commentary and cultural change, and his investments have been a way to build wealth and create opportunities for others.

As we reflect on Nas's journey and the lessons he has shared, we can gain valuable insights and advice for anyone looking to set and achieve their own long-term financial goals. Here are some key takeaways:

1. Start with your values and passions

When it comes to setting financial goals, it's easy to get caught up in the numbers and metrics, such as how much money one wants to make, what rate of return they need to achieve, and how quickly they can grow their portfolio. While these are all important questions, they should not be the only ones asked.

Instead, Nas's journey suggests starting with a deeper reflection on one's own values, passions, and purpose in life. It's important to consider what kind of world we want to live in and what role we want to play in creating that world. Additionally, we should think about the causes and communities that we care about most and how we can use our financial resources to support and empower them.

By grounding our financial goals in a sense of personal mission and meaning, we can ensure that our investments are not just a means to an end but a reflection of who we are and what we stand for. This approach can also lead to greater motivation and satisfaction in our financial journey, knowing that we are working towards something larger than ourselves.

2. Think long-term and holistically

Another key lesson from Nas's investing philosophy is the importance of thinking long-term and holistically about our financial future. Rather than getting caught up in short-term market fluctuations or chasing the latest investment fads, Nas encourages us to take a patient, disciplined approach to building wealth over time.

This means setting realistic, achievable goals that are aligned with our overall financial and life circumstances. It means creating a diversified portfolio that can weather the ups and downs of the market, and that is tailored to our individual risk tolerance and time horizon. And it means taking a comprehensive view of our financial picture, considering not just our investment accounts but also our income, expenses, debt, insurance, and estate planning needs.

By taking a long-term, holistic approach to financial planning, we can create a more stable and resilient foundation for our financial future. We can also avoid the common pitfalls of short-term thinking and emotionally-driven decision making, which can lead to costly mistakes and missed opportunities.

3. Continuously educate yourself and adapt to change

Perhaps one of the most important lessons from Nas's investing journey is the value of continuous learning and adaptation. The world of finance is constantly evolving, with new technologies, regulations, and market conditions emerging all the time. To stay ahead of the curve and make informed investment decisions, it's essential to stay curious, open-minded, and willing to learn from others.

This means reading widely and diversely, seeking out new perspectives and ideas from a range of sources, and staying up-to-date on the latest trends and developments in the industry. It also means being willing to admit when we don't know something, and seeking out the expertise and guidance of trusted advisors and mentors.

At the same time, it's important to remain flexible and adaptable in the face of change. Just as Nas has reinvented himself and his career multiple times over the years, successful investors need to be able to pivot and adjust their strategies as circumstances evolve. This may mean rebalancing our portfolios, exploring new asset classes or investment vehicles, or even rethinking our overall financial goals and priorities.

By embracing a mindset of continuous learning and adaptation, we can position ourselves for long-term success in an ever-changing financial landscape. We can also find greater fulfillment and meaning in the process of growth and discovery itself, knowing that we are always striving to be the best versions of ourselves.

4. Build a strong team and support system

No one achieves financial success alone, and Nas is no exception. Throughout his career, he has surrounded himself with a network of trusted advisors, mentors, and collaborators who have helped him navigate the complexities of the music industry and the investing world. He has also been a mentor and supporter himself, using his platform and resources to uplift and empower others in his community.

The lesson here is clear: building a strong team and support system is essential for achieving our long-term financial goals. This means seeking out the expertise and guidance of financial professionals, such as financial advisors, accountants, and attorneys, who can help us create and implement a comprehensive financial plan. It also means cultivating relationships with peers and mentors who share our values and can offer valuable insights and perspectives.

But building a strong support system is not just about financial matters. It's also about surrounding ourselves with people who believe in us, challenge us to be our best selves, and provide emotional and practical support when we need it most. Whether it's family, friends, or a wider community of like-minded individuals, having a strong network of support can make all the difference in our financial and personal lives.

5. Stay true to your roots and give back

Finally, one of the most inspiring aspects of Nas's investing philosophy is his commitment to staying true to his roots and giving back to his community. Despite his incredible success and wealth, Nas has never forgotten where he came from or the struggles and challenges he faced along the way. Instead, he has used his platform and resources to create opportunities for others and to support the causes and communities he cares about most.

For Nas, this has meant investing in education and youth development programs, supporting Black-owned businesses and entrepreneurs, and using his music and storytelling to shed light on important social and political issues. It has also meant staying connected to his hometown of Queensbridge, and using his success to inspire and empower the next generation of leaders and changemakers.

As we think about our own long-term financial goals, it's important to consider how we can use our resources and talents to make a positive impact on the world around us. This may mean donating to charitable causes, volunteering our time and skills, or investing in socially-responsible companies and initiatives. It may also mean staying connected to our own roots and communities, and using our success to lift up and empower others.

By staying true to our values and giving back to others, we can find greater meaning and fulfillment in our financial journey. We can also create a legacy that extends beyond our own individual achievements, and that contributes to a more just, equitable, and sustainable world for all.

Staying True to Your Roots and Values in Investing

As we've seen throughout this book, investing is not just about making money. It's about aligning our financial goals with our deepest values and aspirations, and using our resources to create the kind of world we want to live in. For Nas, this has meant staying true to his roots in hip-hop culture and the Queensbridge community, while also expanding his horizons and exploring new opportunities in the investing world.

One of the key lessons from Nas's journey is the importance of authenticity and integrity in all aspects of our lives, including our financial decisions. Just as Nas has never compromised his artistic vision or his commitment to social justice, even in the face of commercial pressures or industry expectations, we too must stay true to our own values and principles as we navigate the complex world of investing.

This means being honest with ourselves about what matters most to us, and what kind of impact we want to have on the world. It means doing our due diligence and making informed decisions based on our own research and analysis, rather than simply following the crowd or chasing the latest trends. And it means being willing to stand up for what we believe in, even when it may be unpopular or unconventional.

At the same time, staying true to our roots and values doesn't mean being rigid or inflexible in our approach to investing. Just as Nas has evolved and adapted his music and his business ventures over the years, we too must be willing to learn and grow as we encounter new challenges and opportunities in the market.

This may mean diversifying our portfolios and exploring new asset classes or investment strategies that align with our long-term goals and risk tolerance. It may mean seeking out the guidance and expertise of trusted advisors and mentors who can help us navigate the complexities of the financial world. And it may mean being open to new ideas and perspectives that challenge our assumptions and broaden our horizons.

Ultimately, the key to staying true to our roots and values in investing is to remain grounded in a sense of purpose and intentionality. Rather than simply chasing returns or trying to beat the market, we must stay focused on the bigger picture of what we're trying to achieve and why it matters.

For some of us, this may mean investing in companies and initiatives that are working to solve pressing social and environmental challenges, such as climate change, racial justice, or global health. For others, it may mean supporting local businesses and entrepreneurs who are creating jobs and opportunities in our own communities. And for still others, it may mean building a financial legacy that can support our loved ones and the causes we care about for generations to come.

No matter what our specific goals and values may be, the important thing is to stay true to them in all aspects of our financial lives. By aligning our investments with our deepest beliefs and aspirations, we can find greater meaning and fulfillment in the pursuit of wealth, while also making a positive impact on the world around us.

Of course, staying true to our roots and values in investing is not always easy, especially in a world that often prioritizes short-term gains over long-term sustainability and social responsibility. There may be times when we face pressure to compromise our principles or chase after the latest hot stock or trend, even if it doesn't align with our broader goals and values.

In these moments, it's important to remember the example of leaders like Nas, who have stayed true to their vision and their values even in the face of adversity and temptation. It's important to surround ourselves with a community of like-minded investors and advisors who share our commitment to ethical and socially-responsible investing. And it's important to keep our eyes on the bigger picture of the kind of world we want to create, and the role that our investments can play in bringing that vision to life.

Envisioning Your Financial Future

So what does all of this mean for you, as you chart your own path through the world of investing and personal finance? How can you take the lessons and insights from Nas's journey and apply them to your own unique circumstances and goals?

The first step is to take a step back and reflect on your own values, passions, and purpose in life. What kind of world do you want to live in, and what role do you want to play in creating that world? What are the causes and communities that you care about most, and how can you use your financial resources to support and empower them?

This may involve some deep soul-searching and introspection, as well as conversations with trusted friends, family members, and advisors who can help you clarify your priorities and values. It may also involve doing some research and exploration into different investment options and strategies that align with your goals and risk tolerance.

Once you have a clear sense of your values and priorities, the next step is to start setting specific, measurable goals for your financial future. This may include short-term goals like paying off debt or building an emergency fund, as well as longer-term goals like saving for retirement or creating a legacy for your loved ones.

When setting these goals, it's important to be realistic and achievable, while also stretching yourself to dream big and aim high. You may want to break your goals down into smaller, more manageable steps, and create a timeline and action plan for achieving them over time.

As you work towards your goals, it's also important to stay disciplined and focused, even in the face of market volatility or unexpected setbacks. This may mean creating a budget and sticking to it, automating your savings and investments, and seeking out the guidance and support of trusted advisors and mentors along the way.

At the same time, it's important to remain flexible and adaptable, and to be willing to adjust your strategies and tactics as circumstances change. Just as Nas has reinvented himself and his career multiple times over the years, you too may need to pivot and adjust your approach to investing as new opportunities and challenges arise.

Ultimately, envisioning your financial future is about more than just numbers and spreadsheets. It's about creating a life that is aligned with your deepest values and aspirations, and using your resources to make a positive impact on the world around you.

Whether you're just starting out on your investing journey or you're a seasoned pro, the lessons and insights from Nas's story can provide valuable guidance and inspiration along the way. By staying true to your roots and values, setting clear and meaningful goals, and surrounding yourself with a supportive community of advisors and peers, you can chart your own path to financial success and fulfillment.

So dream big, stay focused, and never lose sight of the bigger picture. With the right mindset and approach, you too can achieve your own version of "If I Ruled the World," and create a financial future that is as rich and meaningful as the life you want to live.

The World is Yours

As we come to the end of this exploration of the art and science of investing, it's worth taking a moment to reflect on the incredible journey that Nas has taken, and the lessons and insights that we can draw from his story.

From his early days as a young rapper in the Queensbridge projects to his later years as a successful entrepreneur and investor, Nas has always been driven by a deep sense of purpose and a desire to create a better world for himself and his community. Through his music, his business ventures, and his philanthropy, he has used his talent and his resources to inspire and empower others, and to make a positive impact on the world around him.

In many ways, Nas embodies the spirit of the true "Illmatic Investor" – someone who approaches the world of finance with creativity, integrity, and a commitment to social justice. He has shown us that investing is not just about making money, but about aligning our resources with our values and using them to create meaningful change in the world.

Whether you're a seasoned investor or just starting out on your financial journey, the lessons and insights from Nas's story can provide valuable guidance and inspiration along the way. By staying true to your roots and values, setting clear and meaningful goals, and surrounding yourself with a supportive community of advisors and peers, you too can achieve your own version of financial success and fulfillment.

But perhaps the most important lesson we can take from Nas's journey is the idea that "the world is yours" – that each of us has the power and the potential to create the kind of life and the kind of world we want to see. Whether it's through our investments, our careers, our relationships, or our communities, we all have the ability to make a positive impact and leave a lasting legacy.

So as you continue on your own path through the world of finance and beyond, remember the words of Nas: "I know I can, be what I wanna be, if I work hard at it, I'll be where I wanna be." With dedication, discipline, and a commitment to your values and your vision, you too can achieve your dreams and make your mark on the world.

And when you look back on your journey years from now, may you be able to say, with pride and satisfaction, that you stayed true to yourself and your ideals, and that you used your talents and your resources to create a better world for yourself and for all those who will come after you. Because in the end, that is the true measure of success – not just in investing, but in life itself.

So go forth with courage, with compassion, and with a sense of purpose. The world is yours, and the future is bright. Embrace it, and make it your own.

APPENDIX A

GLOSSARY OF INVESTMENT TERMS

1. Asset Allocation: The process of dividing your investment portfolio among different asset categories, such as stocks, bonds, and cash.

Example: Jay-Z diversified his portfolio by allocating his assets across various ventures, including his music catalog, real estate, and stakes in companies like Uber and Tidal.

2. Angel Investor: An individual who provides capital for a startup, usually in exchange for convertible debt or ownership equity.

Example: Nas acted as an angel investor when he provided early funding for the hip-hop magazine Mass Appeal in exchange for an ownership stake in the company.

3. Bear Market: A market condition in which the prices of securities are falling, and widespread pessimism causes the negative sentiment to be self-sustaining.

Example: The hip-hop industry experienced a bear market in the late 2000s as album sales declined due to piracy and the shift towards digital streaming.

4. Bond: A debt investment in which an investor loans money to an entity (typically a company or government) that borrows the funds for a defined period at a fixed interest rate.

Example: If Kendrick Lamar invested in a government bond, he would be lending money to the government in exchange for regular interest payments and the return of the principal upon maturity.

5. Bull Market: A market condition in which prices are rising or are expected to rise.

Example: The popularity of hip-hop music in the mainstream during the 1990s and early 2000s created a bull market for hip-hop record labels and artists.

6. Capital Gain: The profit realized when selling an asset for a price higher than the original purchase price.

Example: Dr. Dre realized a significant capital gain when he sold Beats Electronics to Apple for $3 billion in 2014.

7. Capital Markets: Markets where buyers and sellers engage in trade of financial securities like bonds, stocks, and currencies.

Example: Hip-hop artists often engage with capital markets when they list their music catalogs or brands for sale to investors.

8. Diversification: The process of allocating capital in a way that reduces the exposure to any one particular asset or risk.

Example: 50 Cent diversified his income streams beyond music by investing in Vitamin Water, real estate, and film production.

9. Dividend: A portion of a company's earnings paid out regularly to shareholders.

Example: If Kendrick Lamar owned shares in a publicly traded company like Apple, he would receive regular dividends as a shareholder.

10. Equity: The value of an asset less the amount of all liabilities on that asset.

Example: Kanye West's equity in his Yeezy fashion line increased as the brand's value grew and liabilities decreased.

11. Exchange-Traded Fund (ETF): A type of security that tracks an index, sector, commodity, or other asset, but which can be purchased or sold on a stock exchange the same way a regular stock can.

Example: An ETF that tracks the performance of companies involved in the hip-hop industry, such as record labels, streaming services, and clothing brands.

12. Hedge Fund: An investment vehicle that pools capital from a number of investors and invests in securities or other instruments.

Example: A hedge fund that specializes in investing in music catalogs, including the works of famous hip-hop artists.

13. Index: A method to track the performance of a group of assets in a standardized way.

Example: The "Hip-Hop 100" index could track the performance of the top 100 companies involved in the hip-hop industry.

14. Initial Public Offering (IPO): The process of offering shares of a private corporation to the public in a new stock issuance.

Example: If Roc Nation, Jay-Z's entertainment company, were to go public through an IPO, investors could buy shares in the company.

15. Investment Bank: A financial institution that assists individuals, corporations, and governments in raising capital by underwriting and/or acting as the agent in the issuance of securities.

Example: If a hip-hop record label wanted to go public, they might hire an investment bank to help them navigate the IPO process.

16. Liquidity: The degree to which an asset or security can be quickly bought or sold in the market without affecting the asset's price.

Example: Cash is considered a highly liquid asset, while a rare hip-hop vinyl collection may have lower liquidity due to the limited market for buyers.

17. Market Capitalization: The total dollar market value of a company's outstanding shares.

Example: If a hip-hop record label had 1 million outstanding shares trading at $50 each, its market capitalization would be $50 million.

18. Mutual Fund: An investment vehicle made up of a pool of money collected from many investors for the purpose of investing in securities such as stocks, bonds, money market instruments, and other assets.

Example: A mutual fund that focuses on investing in companies that are positively influenced by hip-hop culture and music.

19. Portfolio: A collection of investments held by an investment company, hedge fund, financial institution, or individual.

Example: Pharrell Williams' investment portfolio might include stakes in music streaming services, fashion brands, and real estate.

20. Private Equity Fund: An investment vehicle that raises capital from high-net-worth individuals and institutional investors to invest in private companies or engage in buyouts of public companies.

Example: HarbourView Equity Partners, a New Jersey-based private equity firm founded by a Black Woman (Sherrese Clarke Soares), bought the rights to part of Justin Bieber's music catalog for $40MM which was once owned by Usher.

21. Real Estate Investment Trust (REIT): A company that owns, operates, or finances income-generating real estate.

Example: If Snoop Dogg invested in a REIT that specialized in buying and leasing recording studios, he would be able to earn a share of the rental income generated by the properties.

22. Return on Investment (ROI): A performance measure used to evaluate the efficiency or profitability of an investment or compare the efficiency of a number of different investments.

Example: Eminem's investment in Shady Records had a high ROI as the label discovered and promoted successful artists like 50 Cent and D12.

23. Risk Management: The process of identifying, assessing, and controlling threats to an organization's capital and earnings.

Example: A hip-hop record label might employ risk management strategies to protect against the potential financial impact of an artist's controversial behavior or a decline in music sales.

24. Securities: Tradable financial assets, such as stocks, bonds, and options.

Example: If a hip-hop artist wanted to invest their earnings, they might choose to buy securities such as stocks in a music streaming company or bonds issued by a music publishing firm.

25. Shareholder: An individual, institution, or company that owns shares in a company.

Example: As a shareholder in Tidal, Jay-Z has a financial interest in the success of the music streaming platform.

26. Short Position: A trading technique in which an investor sells shares of borrowed stock in the open market with the expectation of buying them back at a lower price.

Example: If an investor believes that a publicly traded hip-hop clothing company is overvalued, they might take a short position in the stock, hoping to profit from a decline in the share price.

27. Startup: A young company founded by one or more entrepreneurs to develop a unique product or service and bring it to market.

Example: Nas has invested in several startups, including the hip-hop-focused media company Mass Appeal and the crypto trading platform Coinbase.

28. Stock: A type of security that signifies proportionate ownership in the issuing corporation.

Example: If Drake owned stock in a publicly traded music streaming company, he would have proportionate ownership in the company.

29. Stock Market: The collection of markets and exchanges where stocks, bonds, and other securities are traded.

Example: Hip-hop artists who have launched successful business ventures, like Rihanna with Fenty, may eventually see their companies listed on a stock market.

30. Value Investing: An investment strategy where investors seek to buy undervalued stocks that they believe the market has mispriced.

Example: If a hip-hop artist turned investor believes that a music publishing company is undervalued based on its catalog of hit songs, they might employ a value investing strategy and buy shares in the company.

31. Venture Capital: A form of private equity financing that is provided by venture capital firms or funds to startups, early-stage, and emerging companies that have been deemed to have high growth potential.

Example: Andreessen Horowitz, a prominent venture capital firm, invested in Triller, a music-focused social media app popular among hip-hop artists and fans. They also started a16z - The Cultural Leadership Fund (CLF) which is Silicon Valley's first venture capital fund consisting exclusively of Black cultural leaders and organizations committed to Black wealth generation.

32. Volatility: A statistical measure of the dispersion of returns for a given security or market index.

Example: The price of a rare hip-hop NFT (non-fungible token) might experience high volatility due to the speculative nature of the market.

33. Yield: The income return on an investment, such as the interest or dividends received from holding a particular security.

Example: If Megan Thee Stallion invested in a bond that pays a 5% annual interest rate, the yield on her investment would be 5%.

APPENDIX B

NAS'S DISCOGRAPHY AND INVESTMENT TIMELINE

Discography:

1. Illmatic (1994)
2. It Was Written (1996)
3. I Am... (1999)
4. Nastradamus (1999)
5. Stillmatic (2001)
6. God's Son (2002)
7. Street's Disciple (2004)
8. Hip Hop Is Dead (2006)
9. Untitled (2008)
10. Life Is Good (2012)
11. Nasir (2018)
12. King's Disease (2020)
13. King's Disease II (2021)
14. Magic (2021)
15. King's Disease III (2022)
16. Magic 2 (2023)
17. Magic 3 (2023)

Collaboration albums

1. The Album with The Firm (1997)
2. Distant Relatives with Damian Marley (2010)
3. Untitled with DJ Premier (2024)

Investment Timeline:

1. 2013: Invested in Mass Appeal, a media and content company.

2. 2013: Co-founded QueensBridge Venture Partners, a venture capital firm.

3. 2013: Invested in Coinbase, a cryptocurrency exchange platform.

4. 2014: Invested in Lyft, a ride-sharing company.

5. 2014: Invested in Genius, a media and content company.

6. 2015: Invested in Robinhood, a financial services company.

7. 2015: Invested in Casper, a direct-to-consumer mattress and sleep products company.

8. 2016: Invested in Ring, a smart doorbell company (acquired by Amazon in 2018).

9. 2017: Co-founded Koru, a job placement startup.

10. 2018: Invested in LANDR, an automated music mastering platform.

11. 2018: Invested in PlutoVR, a virtual reality startup.

12. 2019: Invested in Impossible Foods, a plant-based meat company.

13. 2019: Invested in Thrive Market, an online grocery store.

14. 2020: Invested in Humbition, a job search platform.

15. 2021: Partnered with Brokerage Firm Avenue Realty Capital to invest in affordable housing and community development projects.

APPENDIX C

ADDITIONAL RESOURCES FOR ASPIRING INVESTORS

1. Books:

a. "The Intelligent Investor" by Benjamin Graham
b. "Common Stocks and Uncommon Profits" by Philip A. Fisher
c. "One Up On Wall Street" by Peter Lynch
d. "The Essays of Warren Buffett: Lessons for Corporate America" by Warren Buffett
e. "The Lean Startup" by Eric Ries

2. Online Courses and Platforms:

a. Hip-Hoponomics University
b. Red Panda Academy
c. Trappers Anonymous
d. Trade and Travel
e. The Black Business School
f. Investopedia Academy
g. Coursera: Investment Management Specialization
h. edX: Introduction to Investments

i. Khan Academy: Finance and Capital Markets
j. Udemy: The Complete Financial Analyst Course

3. Podcasts:

a. "The Ash Cash Show"
b. "Market Mondays" w/ EYL & Ian Dunlap
c. "Trapping Tuesday's" w/ WallStreet Trapper
d. "Stock Up" w/ Larry Jones
e. "The Investor's Podcast"
f. b. "Planet Money" by NPR
g. "Motley Fool Money"
h. "We Study Billionaires" by The Investor's Podcast Network
i. "The Meb Faber Show"

4. Websites and Blogs:

a. Hip-Hoponomics
b. Investopedia
c. The Motley Fool
d. Seeking Alpha
e. NerdWallet
f. The Balance

5. Professional Organizations and Associations:

a. CFA Institute
b. National Venture Capital Association (NVCA)
c. Angel Capital Association (ACA)
d. American Association of Individual Investors (AAII)
e. National Association of Personal Financial Advisors (NAPFA)

These resources provide a wealth of information and education for aspiring investors looking to expand their knowledge and skills in the world of finance and investing. From foundational principles to advanced strategies and analysis, these books, courses, podcasts, websites, and organizations offer valuable insights and guidance for navigating the complex landscape of modern investing.

ACKNOWLEDGMENTS

Writing "The Illmatic Investor" has been an incredible journey, and I am deeply grateful for the support, inspiration, and contributions of the many individuals who have made this book possible.

First and foremost, I want to express my heartfelt gratitude to Nasir "Nas" Jones, whose remarkable journey from the Queensbridge projects to the top of the music and investing world has been the guiding light for this book. Nas's creativity, resilience, and commitment to excellence have been a constant source of inspiration. The insights and experiences he has shared through interviews and his music have been invaluable in shaping the message and content of this book.

I also want to thank the many entrepreneurs, investors, and experts whose knowledge and perspectives have been featured throughout these pages. From the cautionary tale of Elizabeth Holmes and Theranos to the visionary bets of Warren Buffett and Charlie Munger, the case studies and examples in this book have been made possible by the wealth of information available through interviews, articles, and research. I am grateful for the opportunity to learn from their stories and lessons.

Special thanks go to my team at MindRight Money Management, who have been instrumental in bringing this book to life. Their hard work, dedication, and unwavering support have been essential in ensuring that the message and content of this book are as impactful and accessible as possible. I am particularly grateful to my editor, my business partner, my wife, my backbone, my everything, Ameena Exantus, who worked directly with me on this book. Her keen eye for detail and storytelling has helped to refine and elevate the writing throughout these pages.

I also want to acknowledge the many mentors, colleagues, and friends who have supported and inspired me throughout my own journey as a financial educator and entrepreneur. From my early days teaching financial literacy in the South Bronx to my current work as the Hip-Hop Financial Advisor and BookRich™, I have been blessed to be surrounded by a community of individuals who share my passion for empowering people to take control of their financial lives and reach their full potential.

Finally, I want to thank you, the reader, for embarking on this journey with me. Whether you are an aspiring investor just starting out or a seasoned pro looking to take your game to the next level, I hope that the lessons and insights in this book, gathered through extensive research and analysis, will inspire and empower you to pursue your own version of financial success and fulfillment. Remember, the world is yours, and with the right mindset and approach, there is no limit to what you can achieve.

Thank you all for being a part of this incredible journey, and I look forward to continuing to learn and grow together in the years ahead.

With gratitude,

Ash Cash

ABOUT THE AUTHOR

Ash Cash Exantus is one of the world's top financial educators. Dubbed as the Hip-Hop Financial Advisor, he uses a culturally responsive approach in teaching financial literacy, wealth building, and entrepreneurship. He is also a speaker, 6x bestselling author, and creator of the #1 Community for Financial Spirituality. Inside the Abundance Community, he uses ancient spiritual text and universal laws to prove that Abundance is Your Birthright and teaches you how to access that Abundance NOW! Ash is best known for helping people maximize their full potential by giving them the inspiration, tools, and resources needed to live their best lives.

ADDITIONAL BOOKS BY THE AUTHOR

Nipsey Hussle born Ermias Joseph Asghedom is often sited as a rapper and songwriter from Los Angeles, California but he was much more than that. Nipsey was a visionary, entrepreneur, community organizer, real estate investor, cryptocurrency enthusiast, activist, mentor, and so much more. Through his business moves, music, and community activism he was on a mission to teach his community about being fiscally responsible and owning your now and future in order to build wealth.

On March 31, 2019, Nipsey was fatally shot outside his store, Marathon Clothing, and while it may have seemed that he died on that day, the truth is that Nipsey will live FOREVER!

HussleNomics is a book dedicated to the legacy and teachings of Mr. Hussle with a step by step guide on how to implement each principle in your life. Nipsey often preached about the Marathon and as you know in a marathon the baton is often passed to the next runner to pick up where the other left off... HussleNomics is that baton! Long Live Nipsey Hussle! This is just the beginning!

The Wake Up Call: Financial Inspiration Learned from 4:44 + A Step by Step Guide on How to Implement Each Financial Principle, is a book designed to teach African-Americans how to manage money more effectively and how to build generational wealth. Jay-Z's 4:44 is the blueprint to bridging the wealth gap & solving economic inequalities for African-Americans!

Through deciphering all of the financial concepts delivered within the album, readers will be taught about:

- How to Build Credit to Use as Leverage
- How to Spend Money Wisely
- Cooperative Economics and How to Start a Business
- Creating Multiple Streams of Income
- How to Invest Money in Order For it To Grow
- How to Pass Down Wealth to the Next Generation

Kanye West has become one of the most controversial artists of the 21st century. His antics often result in the questioning of his sanity and has many people wondering whether he is a master of publicity, who simply knows how to keep his name in the news or if he really needs professional help.

Despite that, if we study the man himself and remove emotional reactions from what he says or does, there are many things we can learn from Donda Wests' son. Furthermore, if we take a deeper look into Kanye and his antics, we will see a bigger message as it relates to mental health and money.

Making Sense of Kanye is a book designed to teach you how to obtain financial freedom, peace, love, and happiness and how to avoid (or cope with) societal pressures. Using Kanye Wests' misunderstood wisdom, we explore how many of his thoughts coincide with spiritual law and how we can use these laws to live a well-balanced life regardless of economic status. There is no doubt that Mr. West is a musical genius that can sometimes say the wrong things at the wrong time but can we open our minds and allow him to teach us some important aspects of life? This book will show you how!

In “50 Years of Hip-Hop Business: Reclaiming the Beat; The Journey from Exploitation to Empowerment,” we embark on a captivating journey through the heart and soul of hip-hop, where rhythm, rhyme, and business acumen have converged to shape a multi-billion-dollar industry.

This book delves into the history of hip-hop business, chronicling both its successes and the pitfalls of deals that have shaped its trajectory. Yet, “50 Years of Hip-Hop Business” doesn’t just dwell on the past; it looks to the future. It candidly addresses the exploitation that has plagued hip-hop artists, past and present, and navigates the intricacies of 360 deals. It is a call to action, urging artists to take back ownership of their craft and embrace financial freedom, all while ensuring generational wealth for themselves and their families.

As we journey through the highs and lows of hip-hop’s business landscape, this book invites readers to reflect on the lessons learned, the resilience displayed, and the potential for empowerment. It’s a roadmap for a brighter future, where exploitation is replaced by ownership, and where hip-hop’s enduring legacy is not just in its beats but in the wealth it can create for those who crafted its rhythm.”50 Years of Hip-Hop Business: Reclaiming the Beat; The Journey from Exploitation to Empowerment” is a must-read for anyone who loves hip-hop, desires to understand its business intricacies, and envisions a future where artistry and financial empowerment unite.

Ash Exantus better known to the world as Ash Cash is one of the nation's top financial educators. Dubbed as the Financial Motivator, he uses a culturally responsive approach in teaching wealth, entrepreneurship, self-sufficiency, and financial empowerment.

From the Block to the Bank is a story of how a young man born into a low-income family used his circumstance to change the trajectory of his family and community.

Ash was born and raised in a single-parent home in Harlem NYC. He became an entrepreneur at the early age of eight, packing grocery bags at the local supermarket, then graduating by age twelve to selling mixtapes and t-shirts on the famous 125th street as a street vendor.

Ash started his banking career as a teller at the age of nineteen and worked his way up to several promotions. At the tender age of twenty-four, he became a VP at one of the largest banks in the country. At age thirty-one, Ash became one of the youngest CEO's of a federally chartered bank.

Now as a full-time entrepreneur and wealth coach he has touched millions of lives directtly and indirectly and is sharing his story on how to make an impact while making an income.

Mind Right, Money Right: 10 Laws of Financial Freedom, is a book designed to teach you how to effectively manage your personal finances. It shows you how having the right mental attitude and with laser sharp focus, you can have anything you desire in life.

It's an easy to read book that anyone, at any level, can understand. The book's aim is to teach you these 10 proven Laws of Financial Freedom using the stories of wealthy men and women who have used them. This book is especially geared towards anyone who is tired of having a dependency on money and is ready to take some practical steps in order to correct it. Money is power but knowing how to make it work for you is freedom; Mind Right, Money Right will teach you how.

Abundance is Your Birthright: The 9 True Spiritual Beliefs That Will Make You a Millionaire! (And the 9 False Beliefs that Have Kept You Broke) by Ash Cash is a book that will help any faith-based person understand how to access the wealth that has been promised to them by God. Using ancient Spiritual Texts like the

Bible, the Quran, and the Torah, as well as Universal Laws like the Law of Attraction, we give you the Science of Getting Rich so you can access Your Abundance NOW!